HEALING THE DOVE'S WAY

A STUDY OF HOW TO WALK AND BE TAUGHT BY THE HOLY SPIRIT

as taught to

Sheryl Bruce

by the

BOOK THREE: VICTORY OVER WITCHCRAFT

THE DOVE'S WAY MINISTRY, INC.

P. O. BOX 182060 , CASSELBERRY, FL 32718-2060

Trafford rev. 10/28/2011

 www.trafford.com

North America & international
toll-free: 1 888 232 4444 (USA & Canada)
phone: 250 383 6864 ♦ fax: 812 355 4082

Table of Contents

The Prayer

I break, by repentance, this _(name of curse, spirit or pattern)_ over _(name(s) of people you are interceding for)_ back through all generations, all levels of the celestial hierarchy, as it may have come to me and my family from all natural parents, all God-parents, all adopted lines, all blood transfusion lines, all with whom we have become one, all soul mates, all who have ministered to them or to us mentally, physically or spiritually, all prayed, spoken or written curses, our own spoken curses on ourselves, our own sins, all hurts and wounds, by death, by debt, by possessions or by any other way known only in the Heavenlies.

I declare that Jesus became a curse for us, blotting out the handwriting of ordinances that were against us.

I declare all legal holds and bonds are broken by the blood of Jesus Christ.

I now take my place in the heavens with Jesus and command all satanic activity from this curse to cease functioning in our lives and to lose its hold and to be gone from us.

Thank you, Lord, for showing us the roots of this system or curse and for removing the roots as well. I command any companion forces or gatekeeper (guards) forces to identify themselves now.

Chapter One
Forces of Religion

As the first copies of my last book were printed, the "usual" attack on any new ministry project began. God, in His gentle way, began to teach me about these "usual" attacks on ministries.

Obesity Gatekeepers

The first grouping of forces has to do with the force of <u>obesity</u>. Actually, the root of the word obesity means "to eat against". This force is a *devouring force* that wastes, destroys, consumes, stands in the way of, and stands up against the will of God.

The force of obesity works with <u>deprivation</u>. Obesity also likes to "eat up" money. The force of obesity works with the <u>World Ruler of Foolishness</u>, because this force wants us to look only at a person's body (to see if obesity is present). Most obese people have nutritional deficiencies, and obesity, as a force, can be present in skinny people (those who eat anything they want and remain skinny) as well. Obesity lays the groundwork for the second grouping of *judgment spirits*, which will be described in a moment.

The force of obesity wants for people's spiritual condition to be judged by their body size and not by their heart. The force of obesity works with body size to create <u>rivalry</u>, <u>self-rejection</u>, <u>self-hate</u>, and <u>rejection</u>. The force of obesity also works with <u>addiction</u>, so that it will feel as if it can never be conquered. The force of obesity also works with <u>pride</u>, causing the body to swell up, retain water, and will, literally, create a <u>stiff neck</u> (see more later in the chapter on Leviathan).

Along with obesity, are the forces of <u>procurement</u>, <u>murder</u>, <u>death</u>, <u>defilement</u>, <u>malice</u>, <u>hate</u>, <u>adultery</u>, <u>fornication</u>, and <u>familiar spirits</u>. The Bible story of <u>Herod</u>, and his step-daughter <u>Herodias</u>, describes this accompanying system whereby the daughter is used to execute the vengeance of the mother against a minister. The forces of <u>seduction</u>, <u>incest</u>, <u>Isachiah</u>, <u>Hathor</u>, and <u>Hermedes</u> are also companion forces.

Obesity can be present without <u>gluttony</u>, although most obese people secretly think that they are gluttonous. Gluttony does not just want a second helping; it wants whatever is in the refrigerator! Gluttony says, "First I'll eat the hamburger, then the chicken, then the spaghetti," and "Hopefully, there is a sandwich," and "If I'm still hungry, I can go buy this at the store," and "I wonder if there's any dessert?" Gluttony doesn't care whether the foods go together or not. As long as there is anything to be eaten, gluttony wants to eat it! The compelling part of obesity is <u>lust</u>. Obesity, and all of its companions, lodge in a person's "spare tire" or "basketball belly". Inside a person's belly is a "little ball" which the person hangs onto in order to protect their hopes and what little is theirs. Obesity creates layers on top of layers to cover what little bit of hope the person has.

The force of obesity also works with <u>false prophecy</u> to keep the person tired all day, and to keep their eyes wanting to close. The force of obesity also works with the spirits of <u>diet</u> and <u>self-control</u> to make sure you will continue to control your eating and worry over your calorie amounts *after* obesity leaves. *The obesity system is the first gatekeeper to satan himself.* Break the <u>force of obesity as it works with vain imagination</u>.

Holiness and Church Spirits

After obesity leaves, a special grouping of "holiness spirits" will identify themselves. These holiness spirits help obesity to cover a person with judgment.

The <u>holiness spirits</u> want everything to be picture perfect. They are the empty sepulchers described in the Bible. They stir up <u>strife</u> with one word of wondering: "I wonder why her husband is not in church?" or "I wonder why she doesn't come to the altar?" Their purpose is to cause us to judge the outside and to look for the "holes" in a person's life, rather than seeing others with the senses of faith. Holiness spirits become <u>persecution</u> rather than love. The holiness spirits divide asunder.

The first holiness spirit has to do with <u>self-rejection</u>, and says: "You just never know what God will do and, whatever God is going to do, you cannot change." Part of this holiness group says that the only way you can come to God is by <u>trials</u> and <u>tribulations</u>. It says that if you do not bow your knee soon enough to God, there will be a trial, a tribulation, a sickness, or a disaster that will bring you close to God. That thinking hardly corresponds to the drawing power and love of the Holy Spirit!

Related to the trials and tribulations spirit, is the spirit of <u>vengeance</u>. Often times the loud and vociferous delivery of a Pentecostal preacher preaching on repentance, is actually the spirit of vengeance manifesting in his preaching. Many times, this vengeance will keep people from the Gospel.

In a sense, the holiness spirits license the non-Christian to do all the wrong things. The holiness message says: "You are never sure that you can please God and, even if you are holy, God will still punish you through trials, tribulations, and poverty. So, you might as well keep on until the trials come. At least you can have some fun until you are disciplined. Once you are saved, you will have to give up anything fun, anyway."

For some reason, the spirits of <u>odium</u> and <u>opprobrium</u> also need to be broken as you break the hold of these holiness spirits.

The holiness spirits work to keep us <u>ugly</u>. One the one hand, we're told of all of God's blessings, which worldly people often seem to have, yet, on the other hand, we are told not to be worldly. It is very difficult to desire those blessings, and still desire the holiness we want to have, if we are to please God. How do we feel good and pretty, and not be vain? How do we properly steward money, have abundance, and yet, give to all who need? These holiness spirits will immediately tell you that you have crossed the line, as soon as you receive God's blessings and upgrading. They work with <u>lukewarm spirits</u>, here, to keep you in balance. Holiness spirits also work with <u>self-control</u> and <u>self-rejection</u> to create <u>diabetes</u>, <u>metabolic imbalances</u>, and <u>hormonal imbalances</u>.

These holiness spirits will tell women: "Only men or pastors hear from God," or "Only men can pray adequately." (They also tell men the exact opposite.) When the holiness spirits are saying only the other sex can have certain authority or power, the force of <u>seduction</u> is also present. There is also a <u>rebuking spirit</u> that works with <u>holiness judgments</u>. Scripture says: ***Let no man despise you, to rebuke with all authority*** **(Titus 2:15).** The rebuking spirit from God is *not* the same one that rebukes with holiness spirits.

As the holiness spirits, and their judgments, loose their holds, the first part of this persecuting system will break with a sense of physically "not recovering" from the attacks. There will also be a *sense of submission* to forces that are wrong. These forces will try to bring the past experiences in your life, especially the bad ones, into the present. They will try to tell you that the things you have feared the most, or past hurtful experiences, are occurring again. *Forbid* these forces to alternate! In other words, *forbid* them to make the past the present. *Remind* the devil that he has no authority to bring the same hurts and defeats this time.

Often, the force of <u>vengeance</u> will attach itself to one member of the family and will pick incessantly at the Christian through this person. The "picking" never seems to quit. As the rest of the forces in this chapter break, these strongholds will break also. In the interim, *fight* vengeance and holiness spirit judgments by *reminding* them that their judgments will not stand at the judgment seat of Christ and that their judgments are false.

Often times, the next forces to appear will come from your own mouth, especially as you are speaking to those who torment you. They are the forces of <u>doom</u> ("You will never be blessed if you don't shape up, etc."), <u>piety</u> ("I'm so holy, quiet, and submitted."), <u>foreboding</u>, and a sense of <u>enlightenment</u> ("Nothing is real.").

This is the time to break the holds of <u>rebellion</u> as it works with <u>self-righteousness</u>, <u>self-rejection</u>, and <u>self-control</u>. These join forces with doom, piety, foreboding, and enlightenment to cause us to want to solve our problems by our control, our words, and our ways. The rebellion keeps us in our usual patterns, even if those patterns don't have the power to change anyone else for God.

The judgments of holiness are always a <u>rivalry</u> to God's Word and God's Love. *Break* the force of rivalry also. The force of rivalry is a *key strongman*. It often works between parents and children in abuse situations, and in trying to bring someone to Christ. Other forces that work with holiness spirits are <u>stealing</u>, <u>thievery</u>, <u>bastardly</u>, <u>illegitimacy</u>, and <u>stupidity</u>.

The holiness spirits always *twist* ethics and situations to fit their judgments and their experiences (i.e.: it is always someone else's fault and the person who is judging is never wrong). Someone else always has to change when holiness spirits are working. If God's Word says *all* are healed, holiness spirits will say: "all but so and so, because of such and such." Holiness spirits always make God's Word fit the situation, rather than taking authority over the situation so that it fits God's Word.

Next Gatekeepers

The next part of the system begins to look at worldly forces. Note that it is God's good pleasure to give us His Kingdom. It is also God's pleasure to save people by the foolishness of preaching.

Break the forces of <u>pleasure</u> (note Webster's definition), <u>Black Angels</u> (that protect the unsaved, and those in witchcraft, from judgment), <u>God of sports</u>, <u>delight</u> (versus God's joy), <u>allure</u>, <u>frolic</u>, <u>wantonness</u>, <u>mockery</u>, <u>derision</u>, <u>Dagon</u>, the <u>spirit of Delilah</u>, and <u>betrayal</u>.

Black Angel forces work with osmosis to make sure new information is not assimilated into the body of Christ. They work with Satan and Lucifer to call your thoughts "vain imaginations". These forces are all substitutes for God's blessings. They all use love to destroy, rather than to build up (study how Delilah destroyed and used Samson's love for her). They are all substitutes for the wholesomeness of God.

Additional gatekeepers for this section are <u>Bacchus</u>, <u>murmuring</u>, <u>guilt</u>, <u>brutality</u>, and <u>chiding</u>. Jesus took our guilt, therefore we, as Christians, have no business carrying guilt.

This chapter has really begun to look, in detail, at the church versus the world, at Jesus, at Satan, at us as individual Christians, and at the heathen. The forces involved, as this chapter is completed, will also look at how God orders His family, and how the world views family.

It is important to note that satan is not equal to Jesus. Jesus is all powerful and the Son of God. Satan is only an archangel. Just as God has His body (the Church) so does satan have his body (covens, cults, and groups teaching deceit). Just as God has his front line warriors, deliverance workers, intercessors, and pastors, so does satan have his warrior forces, which are designed to persecute, attack, take captives, control wills, destroy, steal and even kill.

God's warriors are to loose the captives, bring salvation, and destroy the works of the evil one. Too many times, we think of our religion as just our daily walk with God. We don't realize that the enemy's forces are constantly working to tear down God's people and God's work.   In essence, the holiness spirits are Satan's controlling ways to create strife in the body of Christ. They also create <u>division</u>, spiritual attacks of vengeance, trials and tribulations on others, and <u>false disciplining spirits</u> (which come from satan).

STUDY
NOTES

Chapter Two
Forces of the Unsaved

These next groups of forces introduce us to satan's front line warriors:

Deceit

Begin by breaking the hold of <u>deceit</u>. This force of deceit is another *key strongman*. We can be deceived. God will provide you with ample examples of deceit in this section. Maybe a doctrine is "too sweet" or "too jarring". Maybe you find something, which you have believed and waged war for, is not coming to pass and you have been deceived about it.

<u>Lying spirits</u> accompany deception. The forces that work with deception and lying spirits include, <u>satan</u> himself, <u>Lucifer</u>, all of his <u>Black Angels</u>, <u>osmosis</u> (forces that move back and forth easily), the <u>curse of Leviathan</u> (note **Job**), <u>Behemoth</u>, the <u>Witches' Sabbath</u> (every Friday), the <u>curse of the seven demons</u>, <u>mind blinding spirits</u>, <u>mind blocking spirits</u>, and the spirits of the <u>Scribes</u> and <u>Pharisees</u> (they see and hear but do not do the Word of God).

Other forces to break, as you tear down the witchcraft strongholds, are <u>self-importance</u>, <u>self-aggrandizement</u>, <u>attention getting forces</u>, and <u>I am most important</u> forces. *Bind* all of these forces to obey the authority you are using from the third heavens.

Witchcraft Control

We are blinded to <u>witchcraft</u> and how close it is to our homes. These next forces, as they are broken, will reveal to you the witchcraft that has influenced your home, your family, and many of the destructions in your life. These forces are very shocking. However, God will bring the victory and the victorious changes are worth the battle. If there has been divorce in your home, these forces will break the roots of that divorce.

First, *break* the spirit of <u>ouanga</u> (pronounced ou-ang-a). This is a voodoo curse (or charm) that causes someone to love another. It forms the seductive core of the witchcraft <u>spirit of divorcement</u>. *Break* the <u>curse of the sacrificial dagger of justice</u> -- the <u>Adjunte</u>. *Break* the <u>curse of evil from all four sides</u> (north, south, east, and west). *Break* all <u>curses of dark evil and darkness</u>. *Break* the <u>curse of Piowackett</u> (darkest evil from the core of the earth). *Break* the hold of <u>Hecate</u>, <u>spirit of the black dove</u>, <u>Italian Horn</u>, <u>spirit of the black cat</u>, <u>excitant forces</u>, <u>habit forming forces</u>, <u>destruction</u>, <u>burning</u>, and <u>false judgment</u>.

After the forces in the above paragraph are broken, it is time to break the following forces with each person's name as God shows you they have affected your family with witchcraft. Use the prayer as follows:

I break all hexes, curses, vexes, whammies, charms, incantations, spells, and the pentagram in which they were spoken, to me, my family, and my prayer list, back through all generations, as they may have come to us by this person (name each person God shows you separately), all natural parents, etc. . . . ..

Each person God shows you will have a witchcraft control spirit working through them. They may not actively be warring for, or with satan, but the witchcraft control spirit will be moving through them. All of the people with whom you've had "personality conflicts" are good starting points. *Ask* God to reveal His Wisdom about this subject to you.

The witchcraft control spirit controls the flesh, and a person's will (if their will has to be involved, why was Saul ever saved?), with all of the forces that would keep our bodies from being healthy, whole, temples for the Living God. To date, we have learned to walk in salvation, in health, in finances, and now, we are learning to take our authority over the natural forces that bind men to Hell and prevent Christians from having the complete victory that God had planned. *This is where we see salvation for our loved ones.*

This particular force of witchcraft control covers our will to live, and often, will attack mightily with the sense of suicide, running away, or escaping. As this force attacks, you will have strong, and long lasting, hot flashes, infections, menstrual problems (*command* hormones and metabolism to come in line), sweating, much confusion and doubt, and possibly, anxiety. As these forces break, you may be moved to a new home where these coverings are not in place. Further forces to break are <u>cannibalism</u>, the <u>mark of the beast</u>, <u>false prophecy</u>, <u>drug holds</u>, <u>nicotine</u>, <u>legion of demons</u>, <u>curse of the dark overlords</u>, and the <u>Illuminati</u>.

These forces are best fought through several techniques. The first is to *loose* every weapon of God on the forces behind the people who are attacking you. *Ask* God to send His Angels (legions of them) to shoot flaming arrows at these forces. *Send* the curse back fifty-fold. *Command* the spirit of cursing to come upon them, as they loved to curse you (see **Psalm 109:17**). *Send* great warrior Angels to pull down the strongholds. *Ask* God to send His fire from Heaven. *Dismiss* all the assignments demons have been given to attack you and other Christians. If they are reprobate, Scripture says to *ask* God to send the Death Angel.

The hardest part of this battle is to *hate the enemy*. We would be kind, and especially understanding, of the logic of the natural forces talking to us before we would take God's judgment and loose it on witchcraft spirits. We would even judge, via holiness spirits, rather than fight these forces. Inside, we almost know that we are afraid of them. It is *imperative* that we hate these forces as much as God does, because they take people to Hell as much as God does. It is important that we hate the persecuting spirits, which kill and destroy

God's people and their witness. This force will loose us just as all the others have, and when it is broken, the attacks on your body and your mind will cease.

Hold tight to the Word of God and to every weapon He has shown you to date. God will be in control, even though it may not feel like either of you are in control. Don't forget to *hold* God accountable for His Word. He either brings victory, or He is a liar! In this battle, there is *total* trust in God, or there is defeat! Much of this battle will be a fight between the two "you's". One "you" will think and say things that you do not agree with. The other "you" will be your heart. Part of you may fight God's victory in this battle. *Ask* God to override you and bring the victory.

The next weapons are to *determine* who is bound to you via witchcraft control, and who has shifted God's judgment of them from themselves to you. Begin to *tell* the tormentors, and the lying spirits, that they are attacking the wrong body. They *must* go to the other person and be used to bring them to salvation. This is especially true of all with whom you have been sexually involved (including ex-spouses). *Break* all sexual sins with the witchcraft control and with the gods behind them. *Send* all judgments (especially illnesses in your body) to the other person for salvation.

In this battle, every religious spirit that talks about God's Will, will reveal themselves to you by saying: "You need to be patient, God isn't ready yet," or "God really intended for this to happen," or "He has good in everything He does, so just submit." What is happening is God's *permissive* Will is involved rather than His *perfect* Will. His perfect Will is for all the strongholds to fall. His perfect will is for the perfect answers.

The god of substitutes works in this battle along with the strong forces of uncertainty and confusion. *Remember* God's will is what He has promised and all you believe in Him for. If you settle for the permissive answers, you will doubt your authority from Him, and eventually, when nothing changes in the natural, you will get frustrated enough to send vengeance again. *Break* the forces of deviousness, false doors (anything the devil can sell you to keep you from taking authority), unconscious mind holds, sixth sense, all secular humanism forces, and an ungrateful spirit.

Another weapon you can use is to *forbid* the devil to use God's weapons against you. He will often take something that God has done and try to turn it against you. *Hide* behind God's shield.

Understand, at this time, the spirit of uncertainty is *not* a minor spirit. It is a *key strongman* in this system of witchcraft control. This force of uncertainty works with forces that cause illnesses of your mouth, teeth, and gums. Uncertainty says: "You don't know how God will work these things, so lay off and wait." As uncertainty (and these next forces we are about to discuss) leave, we will discover that God will tell us exactly *how* to pray and *how* He intends to work the battles out now. The necessary intercession will be taught. For now, stand against uncertainty and "God's time".

Remember, as this chapter progresses, we are standing against <u>witchcraft control</u> (over our wills), <u>deceit</u>, <u>spirits of error</u>, and <u>lying spirits</u>. *Question* every sentence and thought that comes to you and *compare* them with God's perfect Will that says, ***"I have given you authority; I want none to perish."*** As these battles progress our burden for souls will increase.

If witchcraft control binds a person's will, we are looking at satanic will. Satanic will desires to control. God's will is to liberate and set free, and in freedom, to reap obedience and willing bond slaves. Satanic will is for death. God's will is for life. Sometimes, a "<u>What's the use</u>" spirit will try to bring discouragement. You will also hear one that says, "<u>Why don't you just quit?</u>"

When witchcraft control releases answers, it releases them into a permissive will that produces peace, but no change in the natural. This force of witchcraft control works with <u>uncertainty</u> to prevent us from totally trusting *God's complete Word* (we don't expect whatever we ask in His name). When the peace wears out, we either push God or *send* the vengeance (whatever it takes, Lord), which allows witchcraft control to rule.

God *is* in the permissive will and peace, but the *authority* and *certainty* are missing from the role of the believer and it is *not God's best*. We must have praise, aggressive authority, and certainty in this part of the walk to keep from accepting substitutes.

With these lying spirits come the forces of <u>false adoption</u>. God's will is for families to stay together and for children to be raised by their natural parents. However, His permissive will allows for adoption when sin is too abundant. *Break* all <u>false adoption spirits</u>. If there have been miscarriages, children dying, or abortions, *loose* the spirits of the children to Jesus so that the living children will not be forced (spiritually, or unconsciously) to take the deceased baby's place.

The way an adoptive mother views the child's natural mother affects the child's rejection, or self-rejection. *Loose* the child's natural mother from judgments placed on her by the adoptive mother. *Tear down* witchcraft hedges and circles as you begin to intercede for unsaved ones (and all others for whom you begin to intercede).

Uncertain Riches

One of the most powerful forces, for the unsaved, is the trust of <u>uncertain riches</u>. The companion force for uncertain riches is <u>high mindedness</u>. The definition of high mindedness is to have elevated principles and feelings.

This particular force allows ministers to see the whole gospel, but only through the eyes of *their* gift from the Holy Spirit. For example: Those who have the gift of healing see the body and the illness first and tend to focus only on how the illness is revealed through this gift. Those who have the gift of discernment, see all they minister to only through the eyes of discernment, etc.

When high mindedness leaves, God will allow you to see the Holy Spirit moving through the eyes of other gifts.

Other forces that work with uncertain riches are those of <u>false abundance</u>, <u>rejection</u>, <u>self-hate</u> (this force is the part of you that fights the victory in these battles), <u>retardation</u> (abnormal slowness, delays, or holding back), <u>dullness</u>, <u>feeble-minded</u> (lacking strength and vigor), and <u>the evil guard of paradise</u>. The words dull (as well as the Greek root word for high mindedness) both come from words having to do with smoke, or being enveloped by smoke. Retardation helps you decide to settle for substitutes or delayed answers, because it isn't "God's timing".

The next force is that of <u>unworthiness</u>. When this force works with deceitfulness of riches and witchcraft control, it gives goods, belongings, or money to people who entertain unworthiness spirits. This results in a burden of debt. People, who feel unworthy, are in debt to the control. In addition, the witchcraft control spirits expect something in return for their gifts. Many times, people trust in their own unworthiness. If you have received goods or money from people who operate in this system, you may also have received their <u>guilt</u>. *Break* guilt, and *send it back* to them, to bring them to repentance.

When we become worthy, through the blood of Jesus, we can see Jesus as worthy to deliver our unsaved ones and to keep His Word to us. Unworthiness is the <u>god of substitutions</u>, especially as it works with deceit.

Pity

The root word for piety is <u>pity</u>. Pity is a very powerful force. Pity keeps us from aggressively defeating witchcraft control and those forces that keep others from salvation. We "feel sorry" for the person as a substitute for knowing that we can really set them free. Many times, we think, "Poor John, poor whoever, or poor us". This is tough, because it is so hard to minister and pray. Pity is an *excuse* for not setting someone free.

<u>False piety</u> works with pity. The true compassion of the Lord delivers immediately and is very powerful. Pity accomplishes nothing. Many times, your mind will know God's Word about a situation, but your emotions will be pity instead. <u>Fear of rejection</u> and <u>loneliness</u> will keep you from confronting the situation, thus allowing pity to stay.

Those who move in pity, place you in a position where you cannot control, or fix, a situation. Then, they will accuse you of rejecting them when the pity ceases. People who have jealousy, working with witchcraft control, will often reject you and will allow you to see them in situations (alone or with others) where they could be hurt. They use their control to create <u>bitterness</u>, <u>infirmity</u>, <u>rebellion to love</u>, and <u>hate</u> in you. Whenever you are getting angry (feeling jealous anger) because someone you love will not let you help them or stop them in destruction, clear yourself of this system and stop all pity for them.

The forces of pity are also related to <u>scurvy</u>, <u>spongy gums</u>, and <u>loosening of teeth</u>. <u>Audacity</u> works in this group also. <u>Martyrdom</u> works in this system to request pity, or to become super pious and sacrifice much for Jesus.

Leviathan

This mighty beast slows down and stops deliverance (it is described in **Job 41:1; Psalms 74:14; Psalms 104:26**). *Break* the holds of <u>Leviathan</u> with the prayer. *Send* legions of Angels, from the power of the third heavens, to *tear off* his scales, *chop off* his heads, *chop up* his body and *scatter* it over the dry places. I know it sounds gross, but it does marvelous things to bring victory over your unsaved ones.

God may show you different kinds of demons that work with Leviathan, such as: <u>adultery</u>, <u>envy</u>, <u>jealousy</u>, <u>alcoholism</u>, <u>snake charmers</u>, <u>deaf adders</u>, <u>infidelity</u>, <u>disrespect</u>, <u>slothfulness</u>, and <u>debt</u>. As you break the curse of Leviathan, don't be surprised if God shows you the roots, and curses, which cover those who have given you the hardest time, or for those who you have the least desire to pray.

Leviathan works with <u>hate</u>. You will find that these people push you to where you want to hurt, hate, and curse *them*. Usually, you have good reason to feel this way. You, however, must *decide* not to do these things and to *let go* of this hate. Jesus says to love your enemies. *Send* a river of *agape love (God's perfect love)* to each person. *Repent* of this hate. It works with Leviathan to keep the covering over the people you want free.

Leviathan and hate work with <u>curiosity about forbidden and occult things</u>, <u>mind control</u>, <u>pity</u>, <u>idleness</u>, <u>slothfulness</u>, and <u>rebellion</u>. Leviathan and hate are both *prideful spirits* (as is unworthiness), and both cause *swelling and weight gain*. The people who move in these spirits have no fear of God. These spirits also work with <u>mischief</u> and <u>violence</u>. The <u>deaf adder</u>, in this section, stops up ears. *Cast* the adders into the fire and deep pits. <u>Behemoth</u>, <u>fantasy</u>, <u>sexual perversion</u>, and <u>mind control</u> also work with Leviathan forces. Their neck is where the strength is located. <u>Self-will</u> and <u>self-control</u> are the back gatekeepers to this whole system.

<u>Self-control</u>, <u>self-will</u>, <u>self-rejection</u> (causes a mirror image of what should be -- "should" is an irrational word), and all of the spirits that resist control, which include <u>rivalry</u>, <u>strife</u>, <u>addiction</u>, <u>competition</u>, <u>diabetes</u>, <u>trial</u>, <u>tribulations</u>, <u>finances</u> (legalism), <u>persecuting</u>, <u>rejection</u>, <u>torture</u>, <u>pain</u>, <u>bitterness</u>, <u>grievousness</u>, <u>seduction</u>, <u>doubt</u>, <u>unbelief</u>, all matters of <u>infirmity</u> (<u>emphysema</u>, <u>arthritis</u>, <u>cancer</u>, <u>heart disease</u>, <u>obesity</u>, <u>hormones</u>, <u>body cycles</u>, etc.), would prefer for you to think that you must settle for whatever control God might decide to give you. They would prefer that you think you must control them by yourself through diets, medications, doctors, etc. All of these forces would prefer self-control (they have their own self-will -- i.e., cancer cells divide by

STUDY
NOTES

themselves to multiply) over deliverance and Holy Spirit liberty.

Other associated forces that work with Leviathan include <u>voodoo charm of Majo</u>, <u>Saint Catherine</u>, the <u>control and authority of forty-two months</u>, <u>hosts of the fallen Angels with deceit</u>, <u>briars and thorns of serpents</u>, <u>dragon of the sea</u>, <u>blasphemy</u>, <u>666</u>, and the <u>throne of Leviathan</u>.

This is a good time to close all doors, and familiar spirits, to people who feel they have unfinished business with you, even if you feel the business is concluded.

CHAPTER THREE
RELIGIOUS STRONGMEN

This next group of forces introduces us to some of satan's legal bullies:

Unforgiveness

The <u>force of unforgiveness</u> causes unusual manifestations. *Break* unforgiveness with the prayer, especially as it works with all of the forces in this chapter. The Lord will show you how this force has been present between other family members. This force can be a witchcraft covering over you and not just a situation in which you have failed to forgive.

This force of unforgiveness causes an unsaved loved one to do something wrong. You forgive them, then take authority over the stronghold, and love them again. The person will then do something even more unforgivable. Many times, especially with teenagers, you pray about drugs, adultery, alcohol, cursing, etc., but nothing seems to change. The root, here, is the force of unforgiveness. *Speak* the phrase, "I forgive," or "So and so will not be unforgivable any more." Most of the symptoms will change within twenty-

four hours, and they will begin to, at least, acknowledge God again rather quickly. These manifestations are often called rebellion, but they will not leave when called rebellion. The role of fantasy, with unforgiveness, is very strong, here.

The force of unforgiveness demands death to satisfy it. Many feuds, based on this force, are not ended until death has occurred. The force of destruction also works with this force, as do the forces of Osmodeus, Jezebel, and Ahab.

As unforgiveness works with the Jezebellian and Ahab forces, it causes parents to think that their children belong to them until death and, therefore, refuse to release "their children" to their chosen mates for marriage. Thus, no bonding occurs in the marriage and divorce sets in, causing even more unforgiveness. These evil forces continue to cause the mate to listen to the parents' plans over their spouse's plans, and friction becomes the inevitable result.

The forces of romance and sentimentality (look them up in your dictionary) can be substitutes for true bonding. Rivalry also feeds on this group of forces in order to cause rivalry between the families, and the mates, and preventing the flow of the Holy Spirit.

Hypocrisy

This section, on hypocrisy, begins to deal with many powerful, but somewhat hidden, forces. The gatekeeper for hypocrisy is contention. As the force of contention is broken, it feels like "all Hell breaks loose". Don't be intimidated, or surprised, by the force of this group of spirits. Companion forces (check your concordance references) are: <u>malice</u>, <u>guile</u>, <u>envies</u>, <u>evil speaking</u>, <u>error</u>, <u>villainy</u>, <u>lying spirits</u>, <u>destruction</u>, <u>narrow mindedness</u>, <u>arthritis</u>, <u>rebellion</u>, <u>inflexibility</u>, and <u>stubbornness</u>.

Hypocrisy gets its information from the <u>accuser of the brethren</u>, which is a *psychic control spirit*. This spirit allows manifestations of positive change, but no heart salvation occurs, and the changes are not long lasting.

Hypocrisy loves to work with <u>greed</u>. Hypocrisy also works with <u>jealousy</u> in situations where anything takes their belongings, or friends, away (even when Jesus takes them away). Hypocrisy is a *vengeful spirit*. It cannot stand a situation where belongings, or people, are denied to it. At the same time, however, it will refuse what belongings are offered, unless they fit into prior conditions that are controlled, of course, by hypocrisy.

Hypocrisy also works with the <u>fear of abandonment</u>, <u>bitterness</u>, <u>mockery</u>, <u>unbelief</u>, <u>unforgiveness</u>, <u>death</u>, <u>fantasy</u>, and <u>partiality</u>. These forces are often the *root* of colitis and gas. Many forces in the "Dungeons and Dragons" game, and other similar type games, are rooted in hypocrisy.

Please note that the *leaven of the Pharisees* is hypocrisy. It takes very little hypocrisy to ruin the Christian. Remember, although the Lord Jesus Christ gave us authority over hypocrisy, it is the only spirit He wants us to "beware" of.

Hypocrisy works as a *psychic control force*. Hypocrisy is also the *root* of unbelievers who accuse a Christian of error when their own life is full of error and sin. If they know the difference between right and wrong (and they must in order to accuse us), they are heavily controlled by hypocrisy.

As we pursue these next forces, we are dealing with lying forces that say to, or about, a person: "You're not saved, changed, healed, etc., because you don't wish to use your will and be set free." As you begin to understand these forces, and begin to take authority over them, you will know that the person *has* to be set free and that salvation, healing, etc., *has* to occur.

The force of hypocrisy, as it works with self-righteousness, will always "push" us to decide that the person's motives are not right, or that their decisions, or actions, cancelled out our prayers, or that they just do not choose to be set free. If we, as Christians, believe that to be true, we will stop here instead of pursuing our authority all the way through these last forces until our loved ones are set free. Hypocrisy will always call you contentious and/or "bitchy" when you confront the people through which it works.

The forces of contention keep the gospel from being preached. The cords of affliction, and the spirit of entanglement, also cause people to be bound by this force. Christians can be bound by this force via witchcraft control, through their unsaved ones, and will not be able to overcome enough to have victory until it is broken.

The weapon to remember is in **Isaiah 49:25**, where the Lord will contend with those who contend with you. The spirit of proselytizing and Pleiades are also involved, as is the group of false Jesus spirits. The vicarious forces, voyeur forces and false travailing spirits (note the dictionary definition of travail) also work with hypocrisy. Begin to *claim* the Lord Jesus Christ, who sits at the right hand of God Almighty, who was born of the Virgin Mary, who was crucified for our sins, etc., as the Jesus you *know*, and in whose power and authority you are moving.

Barrenness

As hypocrisy and all of its helpers leave, the next force is barrenness. Barrenness has to do with a barren soul, which may or may not be, residing in a barren body.

Read of the women whom the Bible describes as barren: Sara, Rebekka, Rachael, Noah's wife, Hanna, The Shunamite women, and Elizabeth. Note that unbelief is a major part of barrenness. Note that those who received deliverance only in their bodies, stayed cranky, greedy, unbelieving, manipulative, and contentious. Those who were changed in their souls became strong women of faith. Given our choices, we need to be fruitful and multiplying in our souls.

Companion forces include reproach, judgment, and the absence of God's blessing. This force of barrenness wants very much to say that it is a decision of God that you are barren (you have not tithed enough; it is not His time; it is the state He had you born into, etc.). Barrenness is *not* the God we have learned about, whose command was to be fruitful and multiply. God does not tell you to do something you cannot do. As much as this force (which drastically affects family restoration) wants to play God, it is *not* God.

The "bitchy" side of the force of barrenness causes us to always know the way others should live if they are to be right with God and man. Our teenagers, and family members, will rebel against this force in a hurry! Many times, this force, when working through a wife or mother, creates division, and will *blame* the wife and/or mother for it, in order to allow the unsaved family member to stay in hypocrisy and unrighteousness.

This force scatters your power, your ministry, and your defenses. Barrenness also works with waste, frittering, squandering, debt, the waster, destruction, and slothfulness. Barrenness also likes to bask in its own knowledge.

As this force and its helpers leave, a far deeper walk with Jesus, and a clearer understanding of discernment and spiritual truth, will manifest.

The Thief

It should not be surprising if those, for whom you are praying, have gotten nastier, more disrespectful, uglier, more sinful, and more unbelieving. All of the characteristics and manifestations keep telling you that you should "give up praying for people, kick them out of the home, leave them and just walk in your own freedom." All of these answers are traps! The victory is just ahead! Keep pressing on; *determine* that you have the authority and that the devil *must* bow! This is not a time to walk by anything but faith and the rock of Jesus. *Tell* these last forces, over and over, that they *will* leave by the blood and by the name of Jesus.

The <u>thief</u> is the nasty side of sweet sin. It is a lawless spirit that believes the whole world belongs to it and that it can take whatever it desires. The thief comes to steal, kill, and destroy. Therefore, it is the *root of violence.*

The thief works with <u>stubbornness</u>, the <u>fear of stubbornness</u>, <u>cursing in secret</u> (command the hidden things to be known over and over in this battle), <u>high-mindedness</u>, <u>helter skelter</u>, <u>wild blood</u>, <u>perversion</u> and <u>pornography</u>. It perverts the reasoning and the logic of the Word.

The thief has no fear of God, no sense of reality, and no morals (a seared conscience). It seeks the approval of men and peer groups and, often, stops the child from "growing" into an adult. The thief is lazy. <u>Castigation</u> always accompanies the thief, as does <u>Asmodeus</u> (the prince of destruction), and <u>Osmodeus</u> (the prince of lust).

As the thief gets nastier, <u>violence</u> may come forth if you do not bind up its manifestations. *Bind up* the intense <u>anger</u>, <u>hate</u>, <u>murder</u>, and every form of <u>drug and alcohol</u> (cocaine, speed, etc.). These are spirits, and if you *forbid* them to give their benefits to your loved ones' bodies, they can

STUDY NOTES

no longer control those you pray for. *Command* the person's body to sober up, think straight, etc. *Forbid* the drug spirits to give any benefits to the person, or his/her body, and *forbid* their bodies to respond to the drug spirits hold and/or effect. While there can be physical responses to the drug, the *real* power is spiritual. By taking the spiritual holds away, the body is no longer compelled to respond to the drugs.

Additional witchcraft forces include a sorcery pact in which the souls of future generations were committed to the devil in exchange for not growing old or for immortality. The pact was made in blood. *Break* the pact with the prayer.

It is advisable to read the book, "THE SATAN HUNTER" by Thomas W. Wedge with Robert L. Powers (1987 Daring Books, Box 526SH, Canton, Ohio 44714, (216) 454-7519). In this book are listed the powers of Hell (page 223) which include: <u>Satan</u>, <u>Lucifer of the East</u>, <u>Belial</u>, <u>Leviathan</u>, <u>Hebrew of the North</u>, <u>adversary</u>, <u>opposite accuser</u>, <u>Lord of the Flies</u>, and <u>Inferno</u> (represents the South). Solomon, as he became more defiled, became an idol for Satanists. They often use certain incantations attributed to him. *Break* the <u>key of Solomon</u>, <u>lesser keys of Solomon</u>, and the <u>seals of Solomon</u> (page 201-211). Be sure to note Mr. Wedge's appendix for other names.

Chapter Four
Financial Strongmen

This group of tough forces likes to restrict, or cut off your finances by letting you think that the circumstances you are in are deserved. They sit back and watch you self destruct:

Legion

Legion is the *gatekeeper*, and commander-in-chief, for the two thousand we have already broken. Legion is best described by the *Gadarene Demoniac*. He causes self-destruction. He cannot be tamed. He causes clothes to feel uncomfortable and prefers nakedness. He controls the coming and going of all that you have broken, especially recently.

When the Scripture talks about ten thousand enemies at your right and ten thousand at your left consider that it only takes five people who have legion and his troops in their lives on each side of you. When the battle seems like "all Hell has broken out against you", *command* the legion rulers to take their forces and leave. That is why we have been sending out legions of Angels in these last battles. Legion is the gatekeeper for the very last forces we need to overcome.

Poverty

Poverty breaks next. Poverty takes something of little value and makes it appear of great value. It then takes that item and manipulates you by the item's supposed "special ness" by making you think that the love you desire is involved in that item.

Poverty also says: "You may or may not ever have that item." It makes you believe that whoever controls those "special" items controls your love and acceptance. Poverty also works with sentimentality. Poverty manipulates by belongings.

Anti-Christ

The anti-christ brings total rejection, especially to those who are Christians. It does not want to hear about Christ. It will tell you the reason you are not accepted, and the reason your loved ones are not going to be saved, is because you are so reject able. This force often causes tears and the most cutting of heartbreak. Usually, it will take the one thing you have most been believing in God to do and will demonstrate *total defeat* in the natural. This force will then say: "You see, evil always wins," and "Your God is nowhere around!" You will want to agree with it! It will take all of your will and faith to know, and decide by faith, that you are being lied to!

Whatever has just defeated you wants you to forget that, in the issues of Heaven and eternity, evil will not win and God will still bring victory out of the defeat. The purpose of this defeat is to cause you to stop believing for salvation to come to those for whom you have been praying.

God will, at this time, show you who in the family is responsible for the families' salvation (the gatekeeper). You now have the authority to *send* conviction to them for the saving of their families. They need to have the same burden for their family that you have for their family. The Lord will show you the difference between vexation and conviction so that, finally, it is *conviction* that you can send.

The Lord will also help you to understand that the Lord is the same yesterday, today, and forever. When we release the power of the Lord in conviction, healing, etc., through us, on this day, on behalf of the Lord, it is the exact same power released on the cross the day He died. We have faith for what He did on the cross, so we can have faith that He does it today, tomorrow, and forever. We are His instruments for that releasing.

A strong spirit of unbelief, hates faith, and works with the anti-Christ. This is one of the strongest battles we will ever face.

The anti-Christ force works closely with the liar. All of the lies that have been told about you, and your motivations, will surface and break as the liar falls. These are the lies that have been used against you to misrepresent you to those for whom you have been praying. These lies also describe why you should be rejected! They will fall quickly.

The forces we are now breaking, have acted like "the parent" always telling you what a *bad* child you are, were, or have been. You can boldly stand against these lies now!

Debt, Usury

The anti-Christ forces use, and work with, debt and usury to tie up your money flow and to distort you motives financially. The anti-Christ feels like it does not need to pay bills, and it does not need to give honest value for honest value. It wants to find another reason, or distortion, for why it will not pay for what it receives: "The food was poor," or "The Company has a profit margin," or "The thing was covered by insurance," or "You can't get blood out of a turnip."

The anti-Christ forces will not just *say* they do not wish to pay the bill, but will *lie* to themselves about their motives. This group of forces does not like tithing, either. The Illuminati works with this group also.

Loneliness/Rejection

This entire system of the anti-Christ attacks in the areas of receiving love, uniting families, and restoring relationships. The Christian will probably have to take a stand and choose God over their loved ones in this battle. As you do so, God will strengthen His promises to you to deal with them directly and to save them.

The forces of <u>loneliness</u> and <u>rejection</u> will try to weaken your stand, your faith, and your authority. Keep believing, trusting God, and standing. The love on the other side, and the restoring on God's terms instead of on compromising terms, will be worth it. Furthermore, you will be able to pray others under conviction, and into the Kingdom, more quickly after this battle.

If you will make the hard decision to *keep trusting God*, you will finally move into the liberty and strength you have wanted since this book began.

Predestination

<u>Predestination</u>, when used by the <u>anti-Christ</u>, is the devil's external form, and is the image the devil feels he has the right to create. With this force, the unchangeable picture in your mind (of how the devil will win) is being "powered", as it were, by the force of predestination.

The picture of your special ones never returning, the pictures of someone dying, or being on drugs, are all images the anti-Christ has been creating in the natural. *Command* the false images to break. *Ask* the Holy Spirit's image, for that situation, to come in and take the place of the false image. Continue to *ask* the Holy Spirit, every day, to fill that image. We do not have to have that which the anti-Christ has been progressing toward. He does not control the future, or the present. The only predestination for us, and our families, is into salvation.

High praise, the kind that gives glory and honor to Him and worships Him for who He is, helps us in this battle. Ask people to pray strength, wisdom, and joy for you during this time of battling these last forces.

Throughout these battles, the <u>threat of death</u> will come forth from the anti-Christ. *Stand firm* on the grounds that Jesus already died for the person you are praying for. Jesus paid the price the anti-Christ is demanding for, and from, your loved one! Keep *reminding* the anti-Christ that Jesus died for that person, and that he cannot collect twice!

These are rough battles won only by faith in the One who does not lie, the One who will not forsake us, the One who promised that our households would be saved, and the One who does not hurt us. Choose God in the midst of these battles and remember the issues here are for salvation, Heaven, or Hell. (This section of the walk is exclusively by faith because sight will show you and tempt you to defeat). We can be over comers!

Many of these last battles have really required the kind of prayer work and determination that equals *travailing* or praying with you entire mind, body, and soul. Do not be afraid of the travail, or allow it to become so heavy that you forget the faithfulness of your Jesus.

Orion

Predestination, as a group of thoughts, along with other thoughts such as reincarnation, prejudicial sequences of thought, and many worldly thoughts of compromise, are placed in a person's mind by the force of <u>Orion</u>. (I owe some of the knowledge in this section to Win Worley, in his book "<u>Smashing the Hosts of Hell</u>", pages 32+).

Orion's intellectual strongholds form a network over the mind of the unbeliever. This network can be torn asunder by *sending* the Fire of God to burn it out, and by *asking* that the Truth *replace* these networks of thoughts. It will often appear as though the Fire of God has done nothing to these networks of thoughts, which oppose the Truth. However, *continue daily*, and understanding will come forth in the person for whom you are praying.

Orion works with <u>Lucifer</u>, <u>pride</u> (especially <u>Leviathan</u>), <u>false gifts</u>, and <u>soul ties</u>. Orion, which we will be destroying, is the first of the *mind control* spirits associated with the witchcraft spirits that fragment a person's mind and soul (see your concordance and also "<u>Smashing the Hosts of Hell</u>" for more detail). Begin to *command* the Angels to return the fragmented pieces of the person's mind and soul. This warfare is especially important for people whose minds are blocked in major areas, who have learning disabilities, and/or people who just do not seem to be, or sound like, themselves all, or part, of the time.

Command healing to come forth as the fragmentation is put back together and restored.

These forces also work with the forces of <u>Reserpcarian</u> or <u>Rusipacarian</u>, the <u>World Ruler of Thievery</u>, the <u>World Ruler of Hypocrisy</u>, the <u>World Ruler of Resentment</u>, <u>Principality of Dominion</u>, <u>vanishing spirits</u>, <u>Illuminati</u>, <u>bitterness</u>, and <u>worry</u>. Do not forget to look again at many of the <u>Roman Catholic</u> spirits, as they work with Orion, and especially, <u>Mariolatry</u>. Much of the unholy parts of a mother's covering will break in this section. That is to say, that if your mother loves you, she is not perfectly holy, and those parts of her covering for you that are unholy will leave in this section.

𝕴 cannot stress enough, how important it is to hear the thoughts Orion has used to hold captive the person for whom you are praying, and then to *send* the Fire of God over those networks, until the person begins to discern and change.

Chapter Five
Forces of Addiction

These next forces contribute to the high divorce and suicide rates we have in this country:

Worry

Worry is the gatekeeper for the next battle and is very much a *key gatekeeper*. Worry works with rebellion (which is very rebellious itself), the spirit of multiple testings, and pride. Worry also works with the hindering spirits of the past, conformity, forsaking, the curse of alienation, and failure. Worry also works with the terror, of the next systems forces, and uses terror to enforce the reasons to worry. Worry is what opens the psychic channel to hear voices. (Do not forget to check your concordance and dictionary for fail and forsake).

Hectate

Worry is the *gatekeeper* to the force of Hectate. Hectate is a powerful Goddess of the Underworld that is "called up" by witches. Hectate is almost like an *open channel* which the demons of the underworld use to pass through into this world.

Once here, they harm people and carry out the curses. Hectate, in the spirit, looks like the pipe from a person's esophagus to their stomach. Witches form a circle of fire, inside of which is either a six or five pointed star, to "call out" Hectate, and her helpers. They use the words of Morando to bring specific curses to specific people.

The curses for financial problems, via Hectate, include the forces of failure, greed, inadequacy, lack, need, want, debt, poverty, and bankruptcy. The curses for immorality, via Hectate, include Sodom and Gomorrah, Jezebel, Ahab, the curses of whoredoms, Babylon, and degradation. Other forces sent, via Hectate, include murder, resentment, the World Ruler of Thievery, rejection, a Pac-Man type spirit (that has 20 tentacles, and is a devourer), Yahsun, and the Twelve Signs of the Zodiac. *Break* all of these, along with the witches circle, Delphi configuration, pyrami power, and five and six pointed stars. *Break* also, Hectate with the curse that would keep us beggars.

The forces of Hectate work with mind-blocking spirits, and Orion, by making the person think they are innocent or by keeping them ignorant. Stubbornness attaches itself to the will of the person (compare it, in the spirit, to hairspray that sticks in tiny bumps on strands of hair).

Hectate is used, along with the forces of Babylon, to close doors that should be opened. You can feel the *bars* in front of, and around you, when the demons have been sent to close and bar doors. *Crush* the doors and *tear down* the bars by asking God to *send* the Angels to destroy them. This part of Hectate's system will sometimes redirect you to a door that is based on God's vision for you, but the direction will be different from what God has given you. *Make sure* that both the vision and the direction stay the same.

You may want to *amend* you prayers, in the Heavenlies, to include the *binding up* of any demons sent to carry out these curses so that they cannot occur again and/or the demons cannot attempt to carry them out again. Be sure to *cut off* the bands, cords, yokes, and bonds that were placed on you, those you pray for, landlords, property, belongings, careers, etc.

This particular system seems to be one in which God sends giant Angels, the pillar of fire, and, especially, the Blood of the Lamb. *Release* everything, and everyone, from the *holds* of specific witches or warlocks, especially if you know exactly who called up these curses and Hectate. Another weapon is to *continually* repeat, "The Lord Jesus Christ rebukes you." Also, *seal up* the channel in the people it works through. <u>Ulcers</u> work with this channel.

<u>Failure</u> keeps people's words, and the past, "alive" years later. The <u>fear of failure</u> appears here, also. Failure works with the devourer. <u>Martyrdom</u> will work with Hectate, as well as <u>jealousy</u>. Hectate will work with <u>Orion</u> and <u>Lucifer</u> to send substitutes and counterfeits. It will say: "Things will get better," but they seldom do. This is so bitterness and rebellion will stay.

The *back gatekeeper*, which re-invites this system back, is <u>guilt</u>. It is also the gatekeeper for the next system. There is a curse, via Hectate, of guilt. This curse works with <u>shame</u> and <u>embarrassment</u>, and is sent, by others, to cover a person. It feels like a mask covering your face. This shame and guilt often comes from people who reject you. *You* are the person involved, because *they* are not rich or wealthy. <u>Poverty</u> begins to break, here, in a new way. These forces make sure that other people see a helpless failure that is ashamed and guilty. We often submit to these demons, in the next system, out of shame, guilt, or fear of their vengeance.

Other *gatekeepers*, or *transition forces*, include <u>mockery</u>, and the <u>Spirit of Enterprise</u>. Do not be surprised is these are working through several people that are around who also have the **Ahab** and **Jezebel** forces working through them. These people are major influences in the lives of those for who you are praying. *Break* the witchcraft configurations of <u>Ahab</u> and <u>Jezebel</u> spirits. *Scatter* the circles and triangles, then *break* the circle of power from these forces. *Break* the configurations into pieces and *forbid* them to re-form.

Many of the forces, in these last sections cause the people you are praying for to *use love*, especially your love for them, as a weapon against you. *Break* the curse that goes with this behavior.

Addiction

It was amazing to me to realize that I was under the force of <u>addiction</u>, as I had done no drinking over the years, and very little experimentation with illegal drugs. However, addiction, like obesity, works with the <u>World Ruler of Foolishness</u> to keep people from realizing its major role in *mental illness, anti-social personalities, alcoholism* and *drug dependency*. Addiction is the first force that speaks to you with the voice of authority and, by assuming the role of the head, makes you the tail. (Remember the promise that we will be the head and not the tail?).

Addiction causes you to choose what is bad for you. If you choose to do what is right for you, it causes you to be rejected, or else creates so many problems and failures, that you reject doing what is right. Addiction always tries to pull you back into what you have left behind.

If, for some reason, you persist in doing what is right, despite the problems and rejection, addiction will then switch to it's *seductive side* (the sweet side of Pleiades) and offer you what you want, but only on *it's* terms and with *it's* counterfeits and controls. These are the terms of <u>compromise</u>, and this reconciliation is hypocritical. Their offered love, or friendliness, is not genuine. However, you are hard pressed to accuse them, or the system, of <u>hypocrisy</u>, even though your spirit knows that you cannot trust this "sweet side".

Addiction continues to show <u>resentment</u>, <u>bitterness</u>, and <u>anger</u>. It may be surprising to see how deep the resentment and bitterness are in the people who are opposing you, especially if you have really given up your bitterness from the situation. At this point, if you do not respond to the seduction, you become accused of rejection. If you do respond to the seduction, addiction is still in control and can reject you, pulling you back into failure. As you continue to stand fast, it will then attempt to make you feel guilty for winning and for overcoming.

Cast out the spirit of addiction. *Forbid* it to blind your loved ones as it blinded you. *Remind* it that you are a new creature in Christ Jesus, and that it cannot blind the new "you", as it did the old "you".

Orion and rebellion work with addiction, and dementia, by giving you insane thoughts (you could have just one drink, steal one thing, have sex just once, reject just once, etc.). *Look* for these insane thoughts and *forbid* them to ever talk to you again!

Additional forces include the forces of Maalechacrabbim, and the Valley of Scorpions (see **Joshua 15:3**). Do not be surprised at *sharp stings* in your back and in your body. *Tread* on the serpents and scorpions and *send* them back.

There is also a vengeance, or revenge, of addiction that will try to make you afraid, and will attack in any way that it can. *Bind up* the vengeance and revenge. Other forces in this group include: jealousy, addiction to salt (a major demon that brings in many food addictions), fear of discernment, hatred of parents, hatred of men, hatred of women, the stalking spirits of rape, murder, conservator ship, shrew, trolls, gargoyles, gremlins, Anti-Christ, and the higher force as we know him.

(Read "Alcoholics Anonymous", the basic textbook of the group Alcoholics Anonymous, to gain much insight into alcoholism. Understand, that while God uses this channel to begin gathering his flock, Jesus is our salvation and His name is above *all* others. Do not condemn those that choose this path, but encourage them to continue their spiritual growth in Christ. Remember A.A. is not a religion, not does it profess to be. It was given to alcoholics by God, through Bill Wilson and Dr. Bob Smith, to help them return to Him for healing, not as a form of worship).

Addiction works by binding you *exclusively* to itself through loneliness, worry, infirmity, financial reversal forces, sleep, resentment, and by the whole guardian system of failure. There is also the sting of death, a mind blocking spirit, and a fatigue unto death that work with addiction.

The "flesh" forces also appear here. They include the pride of life, lust of the flesh, and lust of the eyes. There may also be a tightening and/or cough in the throat. *Crucify* these forces. They will leave when you order crucifixion for them. The forces in this system often talk to you in *dreams*. *Be careful* of what you listen to from dreams during this phase.

The forces, in this system of addiction, paint a shell, or image, over you for the world to see. They will describe you as dumb, drunk, addict, inept, suicidal, etc., and will attempt to force you to match these descriptions. They hate love and commitments. They give a reverse report, to the outside world, of what is really in your spirit, or of what you really think.

Additional forces include an <u>Oedipus spirit</u>, <u>denial</u>, <u>fretting</u> (this causes ulcers, also), <u>pouting</u>, <u>anger</u>, <u>leprosy</u>, <u>plague</u>, and <u>insecurity</u>. <u>Familiar spirits</u> will try to appear again. <u>Paranoia</u> is a major force that will try to draw you back.

Addiction always promises you answers in the future. It mimics <u>gluttony</u>, and is <u>ravenous</u>. Addiction talks constantly. The <u>rebellion of addiction</u> causes the person to refuse to repent. <u>Insecurity</u>, and the need to only have blessing and money because you worked for them, figures in also. <u>Unworthiness</u> to receive money is judged by the people who have the money to share. Many times, parents, mates, employers, or others (even churches) will decide that you will spend it the wrong way (lack of child support, etc.), and will force the work ethic as a solution. You must spiritually *challenge* this decision by them (that you are unworthy to receive inheritance, or enough to support your family) as the rest is broken. These forces want you to settle for what you have instead of the whole package.

Further forces include a <u>deaf and dumb spirit</u>, <u>thorns</u>, <u>voodoo</u>, <u>persecution</u>, and <u>temptation</u> (addiction sets it's traps, or snares, for you).

Unbelief

The veil of unbelief comes in next. Unbelief is almost like being in a void. It will say that God, your faith, and your prayers mean nothing. There will be no sense of victory, power, accomplishment, or feeling that your prayers accomplish anything at all. Call this force what it is, and continue to *stand fast*, no matter what. *Command* it to detach! This force will use strong lies, terror, and delusions.

Unbelief judges the faithful instead of judging sinners. Unbelief attaches, as a *mind control spirit*, to the pituitary gland. It affects hormones, creates depression, and causes pain throughout various parts of your body. *Send* the spirit of unbelief back to the brain of the person who sent it to you (direct it specifically to the same part of their brain). *Send* it back with the Fire of God to be burned out. The force of unbelief tries to bind all discernment and tries to disarm, or paralyze all weapons so that you cannot hear the discernment, or use your weapons, against it. Don't feel that you have failed, rather, speak *specifically* to the unbelief.

Poverty also works with unbelief. *Speak* to both, and really begin to come against poverty. Poverty will lie, and will tell you that it is too broad to be told to leave, and far too encompassing for "little old you" to make it leave. Lying, stealing, and cheating forces also work with poverty. (During this phase, you may need to invest money to help those who were addicted have what was stolen from them. You may also be attacked, in return, for making light of what the devil stole from them. *Be aware* of this before if happens so you will be able to shield yourself and cast off whatever attack he tries).

The <u>force of compromise</u> works with the unbelief system. It tries to tell you: "If you will give this all up, everything will be okay, again." I will also tell you: "The whole world compromises, so why not?" It will point out all of the compromises you have already had to make to get this far. It will try to tell you that those compromises are going to stay, and that your loved ones, who *are* changing, will never go any further, much less, believe. Compromise tells you how dumb you really are for continuing. *Break* the force of compromise and *stand fast* with more tenacity than ever before, especially in the area of salvation for those you have prayed for.

Infirmity

<u>Infirmity</u> works with unbelief in this whole system of addiction. The infirmity-unbelief bondage is the *root of all chronic diseases*. Those who have learned to walk in healing will be amazed at the power of these demons to withstand the healing power of the Word. For the first time, you will want to say: "I am very sick," or "I feel so sick." This can happen even with those who walk with impeccable faith, and only the Word of God comes out of their mouths.

These forces *will* break, but it may take *several months*. You must *maintain* your position that you are already healed by His stripes, and your body *must* respond to that healing. Infirmity is also the *root of many financial problems*, where your money is "sick". Whenever you feel like saying something is "sick", look for infirmity.

Self-Hate

If you stand tall, to this point, a strong force of self-hate will manifest. Look for it! It will say: "You cannot love, or be loved, because you are so unlovely, fat, dumb, etc." I will certainly tell you: "Restoration cannot occur, and you do not want to love, or be loved."

This force will leave with the prayer and a river of *agape love*. With this will come the accusation that any normal affection, or sexual relationship, is "full of lust". *Do not* allow this force to accuse you of the ugly names, and emotions, for those things that are wholesome and right. At this time, *bind up* any fires, or destruction, that self-hate would use against you.

Rebellion

At long last, rebellion surfaces and manifests as the anger of rejection, the anger of self-hate, the anger of addiction, and also, as unbelief. Rebellion says: "I don't want to do it, and I don't want you to do it either." It operates as a *mind control spirit* that says to the person it controls: "All rules, regulations, and reasons for not doing something are incorrect, especially those that are irrational and discriminating to you. Furthermore, there are ways around all of them. None of them should keep you from anything you deserve, or from any form of *immediate gratification.*"

Any attempts to confront rebellion, rationally, will leave you looking like the "bad guy" who is always wrong. This force of rebellion is often mistaken for strife, because it will bitch, nag, debate, and argue with you (making all of your arguments worthless) until you give in and its demands are met. Rebellion, in the system of addiction, is the behavior of <u>denial,</u> and works closely with <u>covetousness</u> and <u>ungratefulness</u>. The force of rebellion breaks by *anointing* your house, and yourself, with oil.

Obsession

An additional force of <u>obsession</u> will surface near the end of the addiction system. The *gatekeeper* is the force of <u>teasing</u> or <u>goading</u>. As it breaks, an extremely strong force of *sexual arousal* will surface, encouraging you to satisfy it by adultery or by sexual relationships that do not satisfy (even with your mate, where they should satisfy). No one else seems to notice this arousal, and you will want to manipulate whatever is necessary to see it satisfied.

Sexual teasing becomes a major tool, here. It will laugh at you and make fun of the discomfort, and the lengths you think of going to, for its satisfaction, especially if one of the solutions is for you to "pay money for it". This teasing, and laughter, is the *root of pornography and sadomasochism*, which produces painful, but delightful, desires that are never satisfied. If you are a Christian seeking to be faithful to your spouse, or are entering into a new Godly relationship, it will cause you to reject your mate by saying that they are the sender of this seduction or by saying that they cannot satisfy it.

This is a *witchcraft soul curse* that is sent from someone outside the relationship. It is phrased in such a way as to curse you with only short term sexual relationships with no permanence. It is the outsider's way of having a sexual relationship with you without physical contact. This becomes completed, spiritually, if masturbation is used to satisfy the arousal and gives continued control, and access, to your body.

Fantasy, cheating, lying, stealing, and self-hate all accompany this force. It also causes you to see only the parts of your mate's personality that are "non-arousing" and/or "dull", so you will reject them. Your mate's response is to withdraw, become cold-hearted, and angry. They are totally unaware of the situation which causes even more frustration. It will also cause them to feel threatened by you, and by any confrontations you have with them, during this time. The accusation of "being a witch" will break here also.

Fornication, adultery, and sodomy all break at this time. Remember, these are powerful demons using *mind control* -- they are not you. Break, also, the spirit of whoredoms, Babylon, and gigolo and prostitution spirits. Jezebel and Ahab forces also contribute here.

This is the time to *look* at the sexual being that God has created you to be. You will discover that there is a difference between *holy desire* (which is the force God gave for marriage) and *lust*. Note **Genesis 6** which describes the satanic force of <u>obsession</u> then check your concordance for <u>desire</u> and <u>lust</u>. Do not underestimate the seriousness of *releasing* your sexual control to God as one of the last forces of rejection and for major healing releases to God for wholeness.

The force of obsession is a *major strongman* in the areas of unbelief and addiction. Obsession is the *root of the workaholic*, and those people who become so absorbed in a project that they close other people out.

While addiction requires another person to function, obsession operates without anyone else. In fact, when you try to share what you are feeling, under obsession, other people do not perceive the same sensory information that you are receiving. The situation, in the natural, does not match the excitement and "idyllic ness" that your own spirit perceives.

Obsession is a *major force* whose purpose is to mislead you and keep you *scattered* as to the direction your life should take. It is a major force of <u>double-mindedness</u>. On days when it is not in control, you decide not to go the way it is leading you. Within hours, it will resurface and you will decide to go that way anyway. The message is: "It is going to happen anyway and there is no way that you can stop it." Obsession is a *mind control spirit* that almost hammers at your mind with thoughts of whatever connection it is making (i.e.: food, divorce, unbelief, rebellion, behavior you know another person hates (like a spouse), poverty, debt, self-righteousness, jealousy, failure, drugs, sex, luxury, a person, etc.).

Obsession will <u>lie</u>, <u>cheat</u>, <u>steal</u>, or be <u>violent</u> in order to obtain the item it wishes. *Sever* it from all these forces and *break* its holds, bands, bondages, and authority with the prayer. *Command* it to restore. Do not forget that the addiction can be broken, but obsession's thoughts will be the *gatekeeper* for it to re-establish.

Obsession also blocks the hearing of the Lord's voice in a one-on-one relationship, and can bind a prayer language for those who speak in tongues. Be sure you, and the Lord, know what is happening first. Then let others confirm it, rather than letting others confirm it and then taking that as God's voice. Obsession will feed itself by support from outsiders.

The most important significance of seeing these forces break is that these forces keep the unbelievers bound. As they break, the rebellion looses and the unbeliever finally can receive and hear the Word of the Lord in their spirit.

Obsession will also cover you with a sense of *overwhelming* <u>terror</u> and <u>fear</u>. It will feel like "something bad is happening, or going to happen" and will encourage you to try to stop it, or to do something about it quickly. *Do not* run, or try to escape from this force, as it will encourage you to do. *Send* it back fifty fold and *refuse* its holds. *Remind* this force that an attack is *not* a fact and *not* a reality.

Abandonment

Abandonment is the *bridge force* between the addiction system, under the strongman of unbelief, and the major system of the devourer. Abandonment continually asks: "Why won't God do anything?" It comes from the "Please, God!" *begging* position.

Often, abandonment is called unbelief, but it is not going to leave if called unbelief. Abandonment will also manifest as *tears* that do not seem to quit, and which cannot seem to be controlled. This force also works with *death premonitions*, which are actually the fear of the devourer that come along behind abandonment.

Many times, the force of abandonment will say that you cannot send it back or break it like a curse. *Remind* this force of the spirit of adoption that causes you to say, "Abba, Father". You are adopted into Jesus.

Companion forces to abandonment are strife, resentment, bitterness, harassment, and self-pity.

CHAPTER SIX
FORCES OF POVERTY

These forces will take you to the poorhouse, and convince *you* it is because you do not know how the manage money:

Devourer

The <u>devourer</u> is referred to in **Malachi 3:11-15:** *"And I will rebuke the devourer for your sakes, and he shall not destroy the fruits of your ground; yea, they that tempt God are even delivered."* (Note the force of abandonment described as a *financial force* in these three verses). Often, we see it only as related to what we do with material belongings, rather than as a *major root of our personality.*

As this force is broken, it may feel like you have lost your best friend. Sometimes, it feels like you are giving up the very core of who you are and what you have trusted. As this force breaks, many of the very deep feelings of *rejection* and *hurt* will be healed. This force is the *root of snobbery.* The devourer will often keep all of your funds, your affection, and your feelings of security coming from a single channel, or source, so it can control your blessings.

The devourer is the *root of co-dependency relationships* where <u>addiction</u> is also involved. The devourer also works with addiction to create workaholics and debt that seems to be un-payable. The devourer, as it works here, can cause the "straight" person to become almost obsessed with "fixing" their addicted partner so that the people around them, and in the community, will not judge or reject them. Rather than breaking the soul ties with the devourer, and then using the blood of Jesus and the covenant relationship we have with Jesus, the straight partner tries to "control" the natural behaviors of the addicted person and their home relationship. Eventually, the only option they are faced with, is abandoning the addicted party and the financial bonds that go with that person.

The devourer steals all of your money so that there is none for tithing, or offerings, and then tells you that you are "cursed" because *you* do not tithe or give offerings. The devourer works with <u>doubt</u>, <u>unbelief</u>, <u>poverty</u>, and <u>debt</u>. When you finally have enough to tithe, the releasing of the tithe money sets you free. The giving of the offerings are used to break the hold of the devourer from other's lives.

The force of <u>scandal</u> sets off the devourer's attack. When people begin to talk about someone, and especially in the case of the devourer, when a community or church or group begins to talk about someone and their inappropriate social behavior or decisions, they loose the devourer to attack that person. *Condemn* their tongues and *break* this force's hold when the devourer first starts to attack.

Abandonment sets off the strife attack. Strife *projects* the problem to someone else, because the problems are never the fault of the person under addiction. Strife will blind the mind of the person that is being blamed and will send guilt to them. Often, the guilt is accepted because their heart is toward repentance, and they quickly judge themselves. The strife of the devourer sets the person up to fail, then sets everyone else up to try to rescue the person, although there is really no way to successfully rescue them. Strife is often called rebellion, but it will not leave when called rebellion. It will not leave until the devourer is broken.

The devourer along with addiction, are *hidden sins*. They spend most of their time deceiving you into thinking that you do not have them active in your life. They blind your understanding of them. They tell you that you have no control over them, and there is no sense in trying to tell them to leave. They will say: "You are guilty" (even if you have just tithed), or "You are too weak to make us leave," or " You are crazy," or "Don't you dare try to talk to me because I will harm you," or "You cannot directly talk to me or name me." Usually, this force has, indeed, harmed you many times and these things that it says are very believable. *Remind* this force of the Word: *"I have authority over* **all** *the enemy and* **nothing** *shall hurt me."* (**Luke 10:19**).

<u>Mental confusion</u>, <u>mind blinding spirits</u>, and <u>accusations of insanity</u> all accompany this very threatening force. <u>Shooting pains</u>, <u>fatigue</u>, <u>body cramps</u>, and <u>numbness</u> are all physical symptoms that work with the devourer.

The devourer also *accuses* you, as if to say: "Why do you need money?" or "How dare you be in a position to need something from me," or "You expect me to do something about it?" or "Don't you know that I don't do that?"

The devourer negates your covenant legal rights. The devourer *steals* what is legally yours, and he *steals* it through <u>legality</u>. The devourer wants you to see tithes and offerings as your legal duty, involving only material items, rather than as a state of covenant. When Jesus died, He paid the whole price for your prosperity. There comes a point, for people under the control of the devourer, where they will *rebuke* him for stealing tithes and offerings, and the guilt goes to *him* for putting you in the state of sin where you cannot prosper and give. He will <u>blind</u> you to your covenant rights, which are higher rights than he has.

The devourer is bound to money and legalism. Covenant is a state of undeserved blessing, not cursing! Covenant is what Jesus provided because we are part of the new covenant. The devourer wants to keep you only at the *permissive* rights of the Word and Law, and not at covenant rights. The devourer also wants you to have the *permissive* will of God, rather than the covenant, miracle working power of God.

The devil himself, as a personality, hates prosperity and prefers a "not for profit" attitude. He also wants us to have the attitude of "having" to give rather than "wanting" to give out of love. The devil deceives us into not tithing so we will not have prosperity. The blessings, prosperity, wealth, and promotion are from God. The only way the devil can steal them, is by deceiving us not to tithe and give. The devil will even allow us to give rationally, sensibly, or any other way, except joyfully, with full tithes and offerings. The major reason tithing is not taught more is because of our own fear of the devourer's ability to turn man against us. When tithing is taught from the pulpit, the spirit of <u>scandal</u> looses an attack (of the devourer) against the minister, unless all doors are closed to him, his family, and his fellowship.

Strife, and the devourer's mind control, causes everything to "blend together." The people hear, but they do not hear: i.e., people think that it means to "give time" or to "give some" or to "give to people", but not, necessarily, to give to the ministers or to give for the Word. These forces are the *religious spirits* that cause church people to smile at all of the religious issues, but does not allow them to really comprehend the doctrines, and especially the wisdom that affects their rebellions, to doing what The Word says. The devourer is the *false comforter* that comforts Christians, and becomes their best friend, rather than allowing it to be Jesus and the Holy Spirit and their power.

The devourer is a very *proud* spirit who causes people to be very hurt, rejected, humbled, and embarrassed regularly (especially in social settings and at church). Because religious people, and people who love Jesus, can be influenced by the devourer and not have their relationship to Jesus stopped, the devourer will cover many Christians and allow them to be in and around churches. The devourer makes certain that they only hear the permissive, or legalistic, will and that they do not hear the teachings in such a way as to actually know they must live by them.

The devourer also uses <u>debt</u>. Debt is how he finances many of his attacks. He *steals* from God and manipulates money. He also uses drugs, addiction, stealing, fraud, usury, etc. This is also the *root of verbal cursing*. People are cursed with a curse. *"The curse causeless shall not come"*. If you are being attacked, the doors for the devourer are not closed.

This force is the turning point between Christians that worship, see miracles, and *expect* signs, wonders, and impossible events to occur and those Christians that *wish* those things could happen, but will settle for just being a good, church going, Christian. I, personally, believe this force is the strongman that we must *bind* in order to steal people back from Satan.

<u>Greed</u> is a very anxious, high pitched and high pressure force that works with the devourer. It is often called anxiety. It will cause people to pace back and forth. The devourer can be rebuked in the name of Jesus (which is the weapon of

Scripture), and greed can be sent back as a witchcraft curse. *Do not* be told that only God can rebuke the devourer! In the new covenant, the power and authority over *all* the enemy, that Jesus gave us, gives us the right to rebuke the devourer.

The *back gatekeepers* to the devourer are <u>defeat</u>, <u>dissatisfaction</u>, a general sense of <u>everything should be okay, but I still want to be bitchy or unhappy</u>, <u>discouragement</u>, <u>self-rejection</u>, <u>rejection</u>, <u>denial</u>, <u>confusion</u>, <u>laziness</u>, <u>greed</u>, and <u>lust</u>. *Remember*, self-rejection is a very proud demon that tells you to reject yourself. It is *not* something you do. Self-rejection, in this system, causes *self punishment* which includes fatigue and/or shooting pains that do not seem to respond to prayers (especially your own, for yourself and family) and does not respond to prayers from others.

There is often a point that needs to be reached, in speaking to the devourer, where you are not concerned with what you have or have not done. Rather, Jesus paid the price for your inheritance, and the issue finally boils down to your authority over the devourer. He will loose your restoration to include healing of body tissues (regeneration), cash to pay off debts, order and peace at home, and family members that are steadfast in unbelief.

The devourer's most precious weapon (when you finally get serious in overcoming him) is to sell you on *reasonable compromises*: i.e.: "Here is a job, instead of loosing cash *and* a job," or "Here are some hopes for cash in the future, but nothing today." The final issue, in this battle, is simply his loosing of your restoration, and all he has stolen, in response to the power and authority of Jesus Christ that you have. If he can get you to accept any alternatives, because they seem right, he will do so. He will also tell you that if you use this authority, you are taking away God's sovereign Will to do things His way and in His time, and will also tell you, that it is not right for you to know this authority and how to control blessings and curses.

God's Will is for all to be saved and none to perish. God's Will is for the captives to be set free. God's Will is for us to honor, *by use*, the blood bought inheritance His son gave to us. God's Will is for us to use the power He gave us so that we can do *"greater works than these"*. God said, if we would ask, He would tell us how!

The devourer wants you to decide *where* these blessings, money, jobs, etc., are going to come from. That is none of your business, and if you focus on a channel that seems right to you (a job at the mill, or Aunt Susie can loan it to me, etc.), you will give the devourer the option to hold it back. The issue is: the devourer found many, many ways to steal and harm, and now he will have to find many, many ways to restore! How it happens, or through what channels, is *his* problem, and is not the issue.

The devourer will also try to talk you out of your victory by telling you what failures and consequences will come if he doesn't turn loose of your blessings because you have told him to. For example, "If your money doesn't come in, you will have to go back home, be in bankruptcy, go to court, get sick, die, etc."

There can be *no* failure planning! God's Word and authority do *not* fail! If you have not grown to the place where you will *not* accept failure, keep going back to Jesus to remove even more doubt and unbelief and covering from you, until you *know* when you say: "Devourer, I rebuke you, and you will restore today!" and you k*now* that he *will* restore!

This *authority*, in this battle, is the *key to continual victory* from here on out, and the point where you *are* a believer and signs and wonders *must* follow.

Chapter Seven
Forces of Intemperance

This chapter begins the system of <u>abuse</u> and <u>intemperance</u>:

Stubbornness

The *back gatekeepers* to the devourer form a system that arrogantly insulates the non-believer from repentance and from hearing the gospel. This system is comprised of <u>loyalty</u> (false loyalty to everything but Jesus), <u>stubbornness</u>, <u>idolatry</u>, and <u>unworthiness</u>, along with the previously mentioned, <u>rejection</u>, <u>self-rejection</u>, and <u>self-punishment</u>. These forces are the *root* of <u>selfishness</u>.

This system causes a person to do something wrong, such as being selfish or rejecting someone, then causes them to punish their own body with pain (thus administering their own self-punishment). They then will act like nothing wrong ever happened. The forces, here, become the person's closed system: no one else is allowed in, and they will "take care of it" themselves. Along with this come holding <u>grudges</u> (that things didn't go their way) and/or <u>bitterness</u> (that they could not have their way). Because they maintain all of the control (evaluating the situation, acting, punishing, accepting, relating, etc.), intimacy cannot be established and the bond between couples and families never materializes. These forces, together, constitute the system of <u>selfishness</u>.

The system of selfishness works with the forces of <u>undesirable ness</u> and <u>destruction</u>. These forces have much to do with parental rejection and this system is at the *root* of homosexuality. This system *steals* the anointing of the Holy Spirit and the sense of anointing that comes with the Holy Spirit. Many times, teeth and gum problems are related to this system.

The system of selfishness uses the <u>idolatry</u> of one person's approval (often a rejecting parent) to overcome rejection. This process involves internalizing that person's values and standards, and living by those values and standards, so they can give themselves "acceptance" for doing things the way the rejecting person would have wanted them to. In this way, they can accept themselves because they are doing what is right (even if the other person still rejects them). This is known as a *counterfeit coping method* which allows them to deal with their rejection. Secretly, inside, they know that they are still being rejected and that the love they have given themselves is a hypocritical love. They know that the real approval never came.

This force controls the body by emphasizing, or increasing, the things that determine physical undesirability. This system always sets a person up for more failure, and defeat, because the system of the devourer has not been overcome and is still controlling them. These people are often the ones who are most affected by the snobbery of cliques, co-workers, and people who have sufficient funds to live well.

The Wages of Sin are Death

Many of these last forces are the *root of terrible destruction* in our lives. All of the chronic infirmities, and addiction, lead to the death of body cells. The forces of <u>addiction</u>, <u>the devourer</u>, and <u>destruction</u> lead to the death (or damage) of brain cells, and to the death of the entire body. Addiction causes atrophy of the brain. Some growing concerns, in today's world, are the effects of closed head injuries resulting from accidents (especially those involving drivers under the influence of drugs or alcohol) and the effects from strokes. The force of <u>confusion</u> works extensively with the forces in this last chapter, as well as with head injuries and other chronic demyelineating diseases, such as multiple sclerosis.

The major force of destruction, for the strongman of rebellion, is <u>the devourer</u>. The major force of destruction, for the system of unbelief, is <u>addiction</u>. The major force of destruction, for the occult, is the <u>devourer's insanity</u> (which will be discussed later).

Further demonic activity relates to the force of <u>deceit</u>. Deceit also applies to any diseases known to man. The "deceit" is that these are physical problems and physical disabilities. These are *spiritual* attacks made by the *spiritual* forces of destruction and infirmity, along with all of the various forces listed in this book so far. At this level in warfare, the attacks are created by the forces in the last chapter (especially unbelief and infirmity, working along with various other forces) to create defeat and destruction.

Our bodies are subject to the supernatural healing power of the stripes of Jesus. Deceit does not want us to understand, with our minds, how to employ the spiritual power of the Holy Spirit! It would rather we leave the healing to be uncontrollable, varying, and unpredictable. All of these forces of destruction scream that *they* will control us, instead of the power of Christ, in us, controlling *them*!

The force of rebellion causes innocent people to suffer (Note **Joshua 22:20:** *"Did not Achan the son of Zerah commit a trespass in the accursed thing and wrath fell on all the congregation of Israel, and that man perished not alone in his iniquity?"*) Others died along with the rebellious person. **Isaiah 1:12** says that if you rebel, you will be devoured. Scripture talks about a rebellious *house* and a rebellious *people*. Pride and sedition also work with rebellion.

Rebellion is a *family curse*. The effects of the destruction, the mind control, and the mind blinding, cover all members of the family. Because rebellion affects the entire house, or people, the only safety for the innocent (in the Old Testament) was for the rebellious son to be put to death by the elders of the synagogue. Thus, the force operating could not bring destruction to everyone. *Break* the hold of this entire system as a family curse, and/or a people curse, from your home with the prayer. Rebellion and all the forces of selfishness, blind a person to present blessings and to what is being manifested in this moment. The person will be so angry (not seeing what they want to see) that they will miss what their warfare has caused to be manifested. Rebellion challenges the authority of the Word of God. One of the best weapons against rebellion is to *remind* it that the Word of God, which you have been storing in your heart throughout this entire study, is working mightily in you. More will be said about this a little later.

More importantly, this last section on victory over witchcraft explains the forces that are working in so many chronic illnesses, accidents, and natural disasters.

The following steps are included in the process of being overcome by these destructive forces:

One: We really did not believe in the protective power described in **Psalm 91:** *"He that dwelleth in the secret place of the Most High shall abide under the shadow of the Almighty."* In the closing of sin doors to the enemy by prayer, we really did not believe in the concept of **Exodus**, chapters **28** and **29**, that tell us we would be either blessed *or* cursed -- not a combination of both.

Two: To deceive people to see the fleshly side of the attacks, and to empower the idea that the destruction of the flesh (especially the brain), is permanent and non-restorative (physically, financially, and emotionally), are all tied together with fighting the devourer.

Three: Infirmity, unbelief, stubbornness, and worldly knowledge, all *scream* that our faith, or our power, is not enough to control *and* to see restoration.

Often, people known to the family begin to speak from doubt, unbelief, and the permissive Will of God, and add to the effects of the enemy.

Addiction works to keep drugs for pain, or to keep the body addicted to the illness, or to destroy family order. Addiction makes certain that the family's activities *must* revolve around the sick or injured person. All of the forces of rejection, and self-rejection, add to the emotional hurts.

In the case of the head injured person, they feel the covering of the devourer emotionally and will say: "I am not the same person I was before." They will often tell lies, as <u>deceit</u> and <u>lying spirits</u> manifest. They will often curse and use language they have never used before. This will break when the family curse of rebellion is broken.

<u>Epilepsy</u> moves in to tear even more at the person. The devourer begins to strengthen previous demonic strongholds, including alcoholism, stubbornness, rejection, grief, anger, etc. With brain injured people, it is interesting to note that when their behavior brings consequences to them (such as, restraints for out-of-control behavior, or someone hitting them for an offensive remark), they will stop the offensive behavior.

The systems of defeat, dissatisfaction, selfishness, etc., are working here.

The person is covered by <u>rejection</u>, because they often feel that they cannot be attractive, provide for their mates, or because their behavior does not allow them to socialize. The world says you can teach them to compensate, but they cannot be restored to their prior state. <u>Deceit</u>, <u>confusion</u>, and <u>unbelief</u>, as well as <u>addiction</u> and <u>seduction</u>, attach to the brain stem and enforce these lying signs. <u>Destruction</u> manifests in lesions in the brain and in all attacks on brain tissue. <u>Resentments</u> and <u>grumblings</u> abound, and are often the doorkeeper to letting the effects of this whole system return. <u>Strife</u> often creates divisiveness and arguments on top of everything else.

The last area of the devourer's hold is the <u>lust of the flesh</u>. This force is rather unique, in that its purpose is to serve the flesh (to minister to our physical needs). It is the power that says: "We have to do something because this situation could get worse if you keep walking by faith," or "God may do something to take care of it sometime, but for now, we need to take care of this." It is the force that says: "I've been praying for several days, weeks, months, and I am just as miserable now as I was when I started. When do we get the answer anyway?" The flesh says: "No one can pray restoration, and our bodies may, or may not, respond to the prayers that are being prayed. Maybe the anointing will overcome and restoration may, or may not, happen. You never know." This force wants the child of God to diet, take medication, see doctors, etc., so that the flesh will not suffer. Whatever makes life more comfortable, and whatever makes certain we are socially correct so we are not uncomfortable in the community, is called for immediately.

As we battle the lust of the flesh, we find ourselves not responding to people who appear to need comforting emotionally or financially. We do not seem to want to relate to anybody except other over comers. We may be attacked through our sexual relationships (those fulfilling the lust of the flesh often are most defeated in the areas of sexuality, and in the whole area of physical and emotional victory). Our praise, our worship, and the placing of spiritual conversation and spiritual things above daily conversation and needs, will be criticized as not being sensitive to those people who are not as "spiritual" as we are. Our inclusion into family affairs, emotionally, may be challenged by rejection. In people with brain damage, these forces will attach to the metabolic controls to affect weight or heat control in the body.

These attacks may occur while we are standing for manifestations physically, financially, or in other ways that are open to public observation. To the public, these attacks may make us appear as though we are crazy. The message, over-whelmingly, will be defeat. Remember that these forces *must* change and they *must* bow, because Jesus is the same yesterday, today, and forever. Jesus will *not* bow!

You may be accused of only caring about your own needs and comfort. This force will also accuse you of serving your "lusts" when you buy something nice, wear make-up, eat (especially if you are overweight), or have enough cash to pay all of your bills, to tithe, and to give to every good work. It will also be the root of people who use another to satisfy their emotional, physical, or financial needs.

The *weapon* to use for this system is the "anointing". The anointing comes from all the Word you have sown in your spirit and from the Holy Spirit that resides within you. The Holy Spirit that resides within you does not take up an empty hole in your belly (which is separate from all your body cells). The power of the Holy Spirit resides in *every* cell of your body when you see yourself as the complete body, soul, renewed mind, and Holy Spirit. The Holy Spirit within you is *real*, and is the *power of God*! It is the same Spirit that raised Christ from the dead and which quickens your mortal body. It is the same Spirit that is poured out on all *flesh*. It has the same power that comes upon us as the Holy Spirit comes upon us. It is the same authority and power as Jesus. It is the power that is *higher* than the power of destruction. It is the same power to tread upon serpents and scorpions and over *all* the *power* of the *enemy*.

The Holy Spirit that resides within us (the force that motivates our praying in other tongues) can be sent forth by our renewed mind in accordance with His Word. The Word, working inside of us, is empowered by the Holy Spirit to cause manifestations. The Holy Spirit makes certain that the Word does not return void. The Word is the Holy Spirit's weapon (**Ephesians 6**). The Holy Spirit is *our* power to accomplish His Word and His promises to us. *Hold* the Holy Spirit accountable for that healing you have sown the Word for, and for the salvation for which you have stood on the Word. This is the force that *overcomes* satanic self-will and rebellion, and brings them to the King of Kings.

This is the force that the devil told you could not be controlled because, only until God released it to bring someone to Christ, could they be saved. It also tells you that God is doing nothing about your prayers because, prior to breaking these forces in this last section, our motives were not free enough to use this power for God's motives and stay in line with His Word and His Will. We must seek only the Spirit, and sow only to the Spirit, if we are to walk in this power and this victory.

The pride of life and the lust of the eyes will break with this system. They are *demonic forces* rather than something you choose. The Holy Spirit is not just the sweet comforter that is "optional" for us, or just "nice to have around" because he makes us feel good. He is the *power of God* for us to *use* and is the anointing that is available, moment by moment, under the control of our renewed mind, to do God's work here.

If you have sown for the purpose of exalting yourself, receiving for yourself for man's approval, for love, or for any other purpose besides exalting God, this system will reveal it. This system will check your loyalty to God and the walk you have chosen above all! If money, or a family member's or friend's approval, means compromise of what you have walked to date, you will need to go around the mountain. Until you finally *stand* on the fact that it is done because God said it would be done, and you *believe* that the power of God *will* accomplish it (regardless of how you feel), the mountain will not move. Your worship and praise, in the midst of manifested symptoms and circumstances to the contrary, and the *receiving* of answered prayers prior to manifestation, can occur now, and are *proof* that you have sown to the Spirit and not to the flesh. You will reap all that God has promised to you. You will be blessed everywhere, especially in the work of your hands. Failure and defeat rule no more!

As you begin to move in the strength and reality of the Holy Spirit's power, which is yours to command, the force of deliberate <u>lies</u> will manifest, and the devourer's tool of <u>insanity</u> will also attack. It will be very powerful. This force wants you to run away or escape, and wants you to think that you cannot control it. It wants you to be very fearful that you cannot stop it. It wants you to be confused and be aware that you could be going insane or having a nervous breakdown. *Send* the attack back by the fire of God as it is a witchcraft attack, and curse.

The doors are open if you have ever been in the occult, or studied other religions, and you never saw a distinction in all supernatural forces or experiences. You must *distinguish* between the devourer, which is satan's counterfeit power of destruction, and the Holy Spirit, which is God's higher power of restoration. As you *confess* these *are not* all *the same*, or that these are not the same channel, you can close the last door to your body, and your life, to the devourer and can move into a place where you can only be blessed. Witchcraft cannot curse you again, nor can religious spirits accuse you of being in the occult, while you move in the supernatural gifts of the Holy Spirit. You can no longer be cursed with a curse.

You finally have authority over the devourer and can set people free who have been under this covering (those who are unsaved, unbelievers, destroying themselves). Remember, the devourer seeks "whom he may devour". It is our goal to make sure that those we know are not among his victims.

As the devourer, and witchcraft, attempt to bring curses against you (especially physically), your weapon is to *demand* the blessing. The attack must stop. This entire last section has war fared against the forces that comprise the flesh. Finally, our flesh will warfare against us no more. Finally, we can break <u>obesity</u> and know that this force will no longer cause our body to swell. Do not be surprised if you are attacked by tremendous <u>strife</u>, <u>contradiction</u>, <u>grief</u>, <u>bewilderment</u>, and forces that cause you to be deeply hurt. These are the *back gatekeepers* of the force of <u>adultery</u> as it works with the devourer. Break the other forces of the flesh that are listed in Scripture again, as well as nicotine. The victory will just keep getting stronger and sweeter.

𝕰njoy the power of the Holy Spirit that resides within you and is your power to see God's power manifested in the earth.

CHAPTER EIGHT
FORCES OF ABUSE

This section continues the system of intemperance, but goes on to include the system of abuse:

Intemperance

The former section on stubbornness begins, in actuality, the system of intemperance. Intemperance is the strongman that keeps us in other emotional states besides those that are the gifts of the Holy Spirit. Temperance is defined as a form of reasoning. Intemperance is the emotional basis for making decisions. Scripture says ministers are to be temperate. Intemperance can be compared to rebellion in that it does not like to have right or wrong standards. Intemperance deals with the control of passions and motivations. It produces incontinence and a lack of self-control (especially in areas such as eating, spending money, sexuality, etc.).

Other forces in the system of intemperance include prudish-ness, selfishness, regret, pouting, laziness, slothfulness, fraud, bitchiness, jealousy, bitterness, rage, hostility, and uncleanness. A portion of intemperance is involved in the seduction of New Age (other forces in the rest of this section have to do with New Age). Some

New Age forces are <u>Lord Maitreya</u>, <u>Pan</u>, <u>karma</u>, <u>God of the Forces</u>, <u>surfeiting</u>, and <u>vision of light</u> (check your King James Version concordance for references to forces).

Incest

Bitterness and intemperance are the *gatekeepers* for the next system of <u>incest</u>, the <u>stubbornness of incest</u>, and <u>abuse</u>. Incest screams that you will never be believed. It is also the *gatekeeper* force to the <u>abuse</u> and <u>persecution</u> spirits. Incest usually comes in while a person is still a child.

The *weapon* for you to use is to *remind* incest that you were innocent when it overcame you. This system uses a <u>time-altering spirit</u> to make you feel like the helpless child who could not keep from being overcome by the evil. *Tell* the spirit that you are *not* a helpless child and it cannot overcome you now.

The spirit of incest allows demons to cross your boundaries. A person who is under the spirit of incest will talk incessantly and will share intimate details very quickly in conversation. The spirit of incest makes the attacks *very personal* and a personal affront. <u>Starvation</u> often accompanies incest. The spirit of <u>rage</u> accompanies starvation and the spirit of abuse. There is also great <u>fear</u> in this system. *Remind* all demons they cannot cross your boundaries.

Read as many books as possible on children who have been abused in order to understand how this system works. It is impossible to summarize all of this material here. I recommend the books *"Courage to Heal, The Healing Relationship"* (formerly *"Scream Louder"*) and *"Broken Boys, Mending Men"*. It is important to *break* the rejection of incest, which singles-out an abused child, often to be the only one in the family abused.

Companion forces for the system of incest are inadequacy, vengeance, spiritualist spirits, spirits of psychiatry and psychology, infirmity, death, blackmail, debt (incest is part of debt), and deceit. Additional forces include dawdling, ghostly, macabre, lurid, shock, amazement, shame, guilt, and the fear of abandonment.

Narcissism

The next system includes the force of narcissism. It has been defined, in the book *"Working Through Narcissism"* by M. Gear, M. Hill, and E. Liendo (Jason Aronson, Inc., 1981), as the bi-polar disorder based on masochism and sadism; in other words the giving and receiving of pain. I believe this is also the strongman for the spirit of bondage. There is also a lying devil that accompanies this force.

The spirit of narcissism is also the spirit of abuse. When this force is working, one person controls another by the bonding of these two forces of giving and receiving pain and pleasure. If we have been raised in a narcissistic relationship, we learned that we could only reflect those things that the narcissistic parent wanted to see or hear in us. They may not have been consistent and, as soon as we accomplished the goals to show them what they wanted to see, the goals changed. A *major weapon*, here, is to forgive yourself for every time you failed to do, or to be, what you thought was expected of you, and for what you felt you should have been but couldn't be. This frees you from the images and looses changes in the natural. Include here problems with being overweight, handling money, etc.

The *back gatekeeper* to this system is the spirit of failure. Failure is the root of negative behavior and thoughts and the expectation in the narcissistic system. It is the force that always puts a child down, and is related to parental rejection spirits. It is also the force of bankruptcy.

A child's (and an adult's) reaction to these forces include confusion, mind blocking spirits, and a sense that these forces are "God talking to you" (what He says is that the child deserves to be punished, it always bad, and is unworthy). A *fear of accepting blessings* occurs because there is fear of punishment to come (narcissism punishes when we have pleasure). A sense of being vulnerable to being fooled, a sense of being exploited, self-hate, self-blame, a sense of taking care of other's feelings, a sense of needing to fix other's problems and their feelings, and a doubt of your own perceptions, are also included in this system.

There is also much anger at God for his lack of protection and, as this entire system breaks, the feeling that we do not hear from, or feel, God.

Religious spirits will tell us that we have to submit to these forces, loose our anger, and be humble. In actuality, this is where failures take over. We need to *use* our weapons, *call* them by name (the forces hate this), and *remind* them that God is greater than they are. We will *use* our holy anger to defeat them! This is also true when these forces are in our mates and we try to be submissive wives. We can submit to the holy things in our husbands, but tear down the unholy. Otherwise, our mates will just keep failing.

God does not change His reward system. It can not be both ways: i.e., now I am tithing, but am still not being blessed financially. We are *not* scapegoats for other's demonic problems and we will *not* accept their guilt and shame. God never fails! It should be noted that we need to break the spirit of <u>death</u>. Death is the power of the devil to empower infirmity, destruction, addiction, abuse, etc. The Holy Spirit (God's more powerful force) empowers life, resurrection, and restoration. Those who have chronic illnesses, and those who have been abused, find that death stays in the cells of the person afflicted. Death needs to be cursed so it can no longer empower infirmity.

In people who have been abused, their body will show forth pain and memories of how they were abused. The "flashbacks" that occur (these can be visual, auditory, olfactory, or tactile) are part of inner healing, and also part of the time-altering spirits. The "flashbacks" will not be so severe if the warfare is done first, and these spirits are *reminded* that they need not hurt or harass while the memories come back.

Dental problems can be related to oral, sexual abuse and are definitely related to the spirit of failure. The spirit of failure also includes blood clots (brain hemorrhage), atherosclerosis, and the failure of body organs (heart, liver, kidneys, etc.). A sense of betrayal, repulsion, and hard times are also included in this system. The sense of failure is also the *root* of impatience, gambling, pornography, and sexual perversions.

The spirit of failure attacks just when you think you are free and succeeding. It also keeps our projects from completion and delays money. It is also the *root* of migraine headaches.

Many times, when the abuse is severe and chronic, a person will "split". Splitting occurs when one part of the mind and spirit does, and thinks, something else for the purpose of not dealing with what is happening to their body. If the splitting continues, multiple personalities can develop. In deliverance, be sure to address the strongman of each personality, and tear down the spirits of narcissism and failure, that keep the personalities separate.

The spirit of denial will try to say that none of these forces affect me, but they are in our family lines and, as usual, they have spiritual functions that are separate from the natural, sexual functions that we understand. *Break* them as we have broken all other forces.

These forces are an integral part of the spirit of poverty and debt. A complete listing is as follows (some are repeats): <u>bitterness</u>, <u>intemperance</u>, <u>spiritualist spirits</u>, <u>infirmity</u> (chronic illnesses, death), <u>debt</u>, <u>limits</u>, <u>lack</u>, <u>want</u>, <u>need</u>, the <u>devourer</u>, <u>abuse</u>, <u>murder</u>, <u>assault</u>, <u>war</u>, <u>rebellion</u>, <u>uprising</u>, <u>strife</u>, <u>deceit</u>, <u>isolation</u>, <u>incest</u>, <u>mind control</u>, <u>rape</u>, <u>chronic resentments</u> (remember the parable of the worker who resented the late comers from getting a full day's pay?), <u>rejection</u>, <u>incest</u>, <u>rejection of failure</u>, <u>self-punishment</u>, <u>intimidation</u>, <u>Jezebel</u>, <u>Ahab</u>, <u>witchcraft control</u>, <u>embarrassment</u>, <u>addiction</u>, <u>Beelzebub</u>, <u>sexual fantasy</u>, <u>atrophy</u>, <u>eroticize</u>, <u>fear of being discovered</u>, <u>denial</u>, <u>rationalization</u>, <u>amnesia</u>, <u>anger</u>, <u>guilt</u>, <u>betrayal</u>, <u>hate</u>, <u>abortion</u>, <u>repulsion</u>, <u>jealousy</u>, <u>confusion</u>, <u>failure</u>, <u>fear of failure</u>, <u>obesity</u>, <u>fornication</u>, <u>sodomy</u>, <u>perversions</u>, <u>adultery</u>, <u>oral intercourse</u>, <u>doubt</u>, <u>unbelief</u>, <u>self-blame</u>, <u>self-hate</u>, <u>exploitation</u>, <u>embezzlement</u>, <u>splitting</u>, <u>stubbornness of incest</u> (an idolaters spirit), <u>binging and purging eating disorders</u>, <u>Bulimia</u>, and <u>Holiness spirits</u>. These forces comprise the last ones. We can succeed!

These forces also blind unbelievers and, when bound, cause them to finally be open to the Word of God. These are the forces of will that we have always been told cannot change unless a person wishes to change (a favorite line of the spirit of failure).

𝔚e *can* overcome and see our loved ones saved and changed by the power of prayer. We serve the most High God. It is interesting to note that the spirit of failure will question the power you are using when you talk to it. We are using

STUDY
NOTES

the power of Jesus Christ. Failure wants us to use only the Father God and leave the power to Him. New Age can only claim the power of the Father God, and that only by deceit, not reality.

CHAPTER NINE
TREACHERY AND TREASON

As we continue to tear down those forces that call themselves a person's "will", a very major system becomes revealed. This system's *gatekeepers* are mockery and error. Mockery and error, along with the failure system just completed, transition us into these forces that are part of sociopath personalities. More importantly, they lead us into all of the evil forces that affect relationships.

The first two forces, in the system on sociopathic behavior, are treachery and treason. These forces have no accountability to faithfulness (to anyone or anything) and they cannot be trusted. For people who have trouble having faith, or being faithful, this system needs to be broken.

Next, are the lying spirits. Do a concordance check on lying forces. Note that lies cause error. People who know the Word of God but do not live it are possessed with a lying spirit (or covering, or inheritance). Combined with treachery and treason, people in this system can lie to anyone about anything. They have no sense that they are lying, nor do they have any sense of guilt or shame for the consequences that occur because their lies are believed and acted upon.

Vanity accompanies lies, as do slander, deceit, and hypocrisy. Because liars always believe their needs come first, others must cooperate with them by becoming martyrs. The martyrdom spirit convinces a sociopathic victim to take care of the sociopath first. Many times, these martyrdom thoughts come out of the system of abuse or from religious spirits.

Next in line are the forces of wickedness (they play a part in personal relationships). The include mischief, murder, manslayers, perverseness, robbery, thievery, unjust weights, embezzlement, fraud, seduction, narcissism, incest, abuse, suicide, naughtiness, lust, rape, abortion, adultery, fornication, malice, sadomasochistic forces, whoredoms, men stealers, whoremongers, insanity, selfishness (see stubbornness and intemperance systems previously covered), sowing discord, covenants with death and hell, defiled with blood, iniquity, strife, lewdness, malignity, and bestiality.

The *manifestations* of people who are in this system include a lack of remorse, the ability to make victims, and others, believe they are innocent, a spirit of charm, and a lack of sensing relationships between themselves and others. They obey their own desires and, indeed, do the acts of their father Satan. For more information on sociopaths, I suggest the articles or books at your local library.

This whole system of treachery and treason often describes the unbelievers before they are saved. It is definitely the *key system* to seeing restoration in families and seeing the first manifestations of salvation in those resisting salvation.

Chapter Ten
Unbelief - Division - Mammon

As the forces in chapter nine began to break, the presence of a *controlling force* that could bring in any of the strongmen at its will and make us feel like we were in a new or repeated battle began to be revealed. In actuality, there were three forces that emerged together: they were <u>unbelief</u>, <u>division</u>, and <u>Mammon</u>.

Unbelief came to the surface while I was studying about *multiple personalities*. In essence, when unbelief attacks a person's mind and spirit, it *fragments* them. It also works with *time altering spirits* to either take them to a time when they were a child or to another personality. The key description is: when an event would occur in a person's life, which supposedly had more than one personality, there would be "cues" to call forth the new personality. Unbelief is the force that keeps the separate personalities from being revealed to each other and/or from being integrated.

I discovered that when I would be standing for money, a situation would arise whereby my helpless child felt rejected. This caused the battle for money to be neglected or forgotten. When the spirit of unbelief was broken, and each time I realized that I had been "time altered" to another part of my life, I *looked* for the "cue", *commanded* unbelief not to fragment me, *declared* that I was not a helpless child, and *refused* to become divided in my spirit, my soul, and my body. I also discovered that the force of <u>incest</u> allowed these presenting forces of unbelief entrance into my body. They would stop physically attacking when *reminded* that incest was broken, and they were no longer able to invade my body.

This force of unbelief can be an *inherited* spirit of unbelief, wherein the family of the person involved either did not believe in Jesus Christ as our savior, the Holy Spirit and His power and presence for today, or in God the Father. *Break* especially, the <u>inherited spirit of unbelief</u>.

Unbelief also causes us to question whether or not we know God's Will, despite His clearly written Word. It is imperative that we *stand* on His Word and His expressed Will for us in His Word, regardless of our feelings of what "seems right", according to circumstances or experiences. Anytime something does not want to "believe" the Word of God, you are dealing with unbelief.

With these weapons, the spirit of <u>division</u> becomes manifest. The spirit of division is a very powerful force that protects the force of unbelief. Check you concordance for division, and read the verses, and context, of each place that it occurs in Scripture. The force of division also protects the forces of <u>murder</u> and <u>hate</u>.

People under the covering of division attempt to make a Godly person (especially one who believes for miracles and who actively does the work of the Holy Spirit) feel <u>ashamed</u>, <u>guilty</u>, and <u>isolated</u> from church, family, friends, and especially, intimacy. People who use the force of division make Godly Christians feel like they are in error or that they have done something terribly wrong (even though they don't know what they did except try to serve God).

The force of division separates husbands from wives and children from families. If someone has not been involved with their families for many years, this force is *key* in their freedom to see them and overcome. Division also attempts to separate mind from soul and spirit from body (Jesus dwells in the whole person). Division also separates ministers with different gifts and callings and separates the Word of God from the Love of God.

As these forces break, many feelings of <u>insecurity</u> (especially in social settings, church groups, and in fearing the calls to the ministry) will vanish. An improved sense of self-esteem will emerge, along with a new sense of wholeness. This force always says: "I don't want to be around those people." It also stops the force of hospitality.

There is a <u>pride of division</u> that also needs to be broken. The first weapon, against the forces of division, is to *remind* them that they are worse than the forces of witchcraft because they are coming from Christian, against Christian. These forces like to deceive Christians that they are doing God's work. That will stop most of the attacks.

The third force that manifested as a controlling force was <u>Mammon</u>. This force is the force of cash. Little can be done for God without cash; therefore Mammon wants to keep all of your cash. The Word of God describes restoration when the covenant people turn back from their wicked ways. Covenant makes God's people exceedingly wealthy (Note the Jews, Abraham, Issac, and even the Arabs, who also received the promise of covenant). We have been grafted into covenant through Jesus' death. We can *claim* exceeding wealth and restoration of body parts that were previously destroyed (especially when we have been cleansed throughout our family lines). Every miraculous healing involves restoration.

The spirit of division says we cannot be grafted in, and Mammon says it does not have to restore. Mammon often portrays himself as a "god" and, when working with unbelief and division, says to you: "If you take authority over money, you are usurping God's place and should, therefore, be attacked, feel guilty, and stay in poverty." Nothing is further from God's Word! We have been promised restoration and we have authority over *all* the enemy (Note the Scriptures that say we cannot serve both God and Mammon).

As these three controlling spirits fall, there will be little choice but to be *fully committed* to God, to belief, to unity, and to love. A sense of soberness will also come forth. Remember, some of the forces that are screaming at you about claiming your exceedingly wealthy inheritance of Abraham (that you have been grafted into), are those of the Jewish race, and other covenant races, that do not want to share their inheritance with you. This is your *weapon* sentence against these forces!

EPILOGUE
THE BLESSING

I know that I will battle and wrestle with powers and principalities as long as I live on this earth. So will you, especially if you have come this far. However, the purpose of this book, and these teachings, are to equip you with all of your weapons and with the knowledge to see healing, financial victory, salvation, and restoration ruling and reigning, with a family line of righteousness replacing a family line of unrighteousness.

By this time, these goals have been met. In addition, you now know how to walk in the Holy Spirit and how to warfare for Him who was, who is, and who will continue to be. I am certain that parts of this book represent statements of limited knowledge, or other things that those more knowledgeable than I will say are *not* Scriptural! The least I can say is that the Holy Spirit was showing me in ways I could hear at each stage along the way, and while I was still under various unholy coverings. These writings are designed to minister to others under similar coverings, not to theological debates. The most I can say is that I have been faithful to warfare and to try to teach as my Lord commanded me. The Holy Spirit will, I know, continue to lead and guide you in all Truth.

I wish you Godspeed and God Bless

ABOUT THE AUTHOR

Sheryl Bruce holds a master's degree from the University of Wyoming in the area of Interpersonal Communications (a counseling degree based on communication theory). She has worked for the State of Florida Department of Rehabilitation for over eight years as a counselor and has achieved the designation of Certified Rehabilitation Counselor (CRC). Sheryl is also ordained through the Gospel Crusade of Bradenton, Florida as a minister of the Gospel. She has a total of 35 years of counseling experience.

The books that make up HEALING THE DOVE'S WAY: *"First Battles"*, *"More Inhabitants of the Land"*, *"Victory Over Witchcraft"*, *and "Final Battles: Financial Strongmen"*, came out of Sheryl's own walk of faith, where, over several years, every demon imaginable tried to destroy her. There were times, during that walk, that others had to help her dress so that she might go to work in order to support herself and her children. She is the mother of two, and grandmother of seven.

Her testimony is both inspirational and touching. This amazing woman paid a price to gain for the world a method of personal warfare that has the ability to change lives forever. To listen to her struggles, you have to ask yourself why she stayed the course. Only someone with great faith in God's grace, and the courage to take on satan's army, would have even begun the walk.

The Dove's Way Ministry is actively involved in setting God's people free through individual counseling. You can visit The Dove's Way Ministry website at: *www.doveswayministry.com* or contact them via email at: *doveswayministry@aol.com*.